ACADEMY
FORUM
First of a Series

HOW SAFE IS SAFE?

The Design of Policy on Drugs and Food Additives

NATIONAL ACADEMY OF SCIENCES
Washington, D.C.
1974

This Academy Forum received support from:

    NATIONAL ACADEMY OF SCIENCES, Project Initiation and Development Fund

    PETER C. CORNELL TRUST

    CHARLES F. KETTERING FOUNDATION

    ALFRED P. SLOAN FOUNDATION

International Standard Book Number   0-309-02222-3

Library of Congress Catalog Card Number   74-5981

Available from

Printing and Publishing Office
National Academy of Sciences
2101 Constitution Ave.
Washington, D.C. 20418

Printed in the United States of America

FOREWORD

This is a book developed from the Forum held at the National Academy of Sciences on May 15, 1973, when approximately four hundred people came together to discuss the design of policy on drugs and food additives. It depicts the successes as well as the failures of communication around a controversial subject explored in a public arena. For that reason, the delineation of the process may prove to be as useful as the substance of this product. The book does not pretend to be a definitive text. It does present, however, a very real sense of where we are with respect to policy and fact in clarifying many of the problem areas surrounding the subject.

The design of the Academy Forum rests on the proposition that effective policy must recognize the interests and aspirations of all relevant constituencies. The corollary to this proposition is that effective policy can be developed principally in those areas where those factors conjoin and overlap. It is hoped that areas of disjunction will usefully define arenas for further research, exploration, and discussion.

The thoughtful and largely uncontentious temper of the Forum meeting was consonant with its purpose of illuminating highly controversial issues. Judgment of the value and implications of the conjunction and disjunction distilled in the Forum process we leave to the reader and to all who participate in policy matters.

Robert R. White
Director

Science and the good life have been uneasy companions in the onward march of civilization. At times they have moved so harmoniously that no one would question that they were headed toward the same horizon; at others their goals have seemed antithetical. Some of the difficulty resides, of course, in definitions. Science can mean technology or the search for truth. The good life can mean material success or moral values.

At one extreme there is a variance in philosophical bases. Science seeks truth, objective truth, and believes that "the truth will set man free." But truth is not always comfortable, and sometimes so-called objective truth conflicts with the mores of society whether they be based on divine authority or the will of the majority.

At the other extreme there is a conflict of practicality. Technology has added to the control of man over his environment and thus increased the good life in the sense of material success. However, as the earth becomes more crowded and its resources more scarce, the blessings of technology to some portions of society frequently bring the curses of technology to others.

Between these extremes there is an even more complex area, one in which a technological advance is neither good nor bad per se, but is to be accepted or rejected if the risks and benefits can be ascertained in some "objective" manner. In this middle area both practical benefits and moral risks must be assessed even though no procedure has been devised for finding a common denominator for these two value systems. It is this middle area, where some of the most serious controversies of our time reside, which the Academy Forum hopes to illuminate.

An appreciation of this dichotomy is of great importance to any consideration of the design of policy on drugs and food additives. How does one balance the

degree of benefit to future generations of a new drug against the degree of risk
to the volunteers in its clinical trial? How does one assess the values of many
apparently useful drugs against the remote possibility of their ultimate damage?
Or how does a regulatory agency make a decision when the research on benefits and
risks of a given product is incomplete even though it is being used extensively.
These questions involve both scientific expertise and philosophical principles.

The subject first discussed by the Academy Forum General Advisory Committee,
the membership of which is listed in the back of this book, was whether there was
a need for an additional mechanism to explore issues such as those described above.
Two general types of meetings already were prevalent. One was the congressional
committee type in which specialists appeared seriatim to be questioned by lay
authorities. The other was a public meeting in which advocates of opposing positions engaged in polemic discussion. It seemed to us that a contribution could be
made by a new type of meeting which introduced adversaries within an environment
of expertise and thoughtful interrogation.

To plan the first forum on drugs and food additives, the Program Committee,
which also is listed in the back of the book, met and developed this format:
a group of speakers representing a wide range of viewpoints; a panel for inquiry
made up of members of the Academy, interrogators of a general competence with no
particular prejudice in the field under examination; a group of invited discussants
from a spectrum of interests and who had such expertise as to prod the discussion;
and a general audience of concerned citizens. Announcements were sent to almost
one thousand representatives of the legislative, executive, and judicial branches
of government, to the press, the legal profession, scientists, economists,
consumer groups, and the general public. There was no expectation that the
problems inherent in the subject could be "solved" in a one-day session, but it

was hoped that the combination of a constructive atmosphere and the format would lead to creative new approaches to the decision making process. I believe that this hope was realized.

However, we may not have been as original as we thought ourselves. It was with some chagrin and a great deal of amusement that I read of a certain chemist-lecturer by the name of Colton who, in 1844, apparently had seized on almost all of the essentials we had so laboriously deduced. Mr. Colton toured the country in the last century giving public lectures for the cost of twenty-five cents on a chemical substance called nitrous oxide or laughing gas. Before giving one of his talks he would circulate an advertisement, one of which read as follows:

> A grand exhibition of the effects produced by inhaling nitrous oxide, exhilarating or laughing gas, will be given at Union Hall this evening, December 10, 1844. Forty gallons of gas will be prepared and administered to all of the audience who desire to inhale it. Twelve young men have volunteered to inhale the gas to commence the entertainment. Eight strong men are engaged to occupy the front seats to protect those under the influence of the gas from injuring themselves or others. This course is adopted that no apprehension of danger may be entertained. Probably no one will attempt to fight. The effect of the gas is to make those who inhale it either laugh, sing, dance, speak, or fight, according to the leading trait of their character. They seem to retain consciousness enough not to say or do that which they would have occasion to regret.
>
> This gas will be administered only to gentlemen of the first respectability. The object is to make the entertainment in every respect a genteel affair.

You will note that we have provided five young men to commence the entertainment with presentations of their viewpoints. We have strong men on our panel to protect our audience from injury by careful probing of controversial statements. We also have a collection of informed discussants who laugh, speak, or fight, but

do not do anything which they would have occasion to regret. Finally, we have
an audience of the first respectability. It also turned out to be a genteel
affair.

                                   Daniel E. Koshland, Jr.
                                   Program Chairman

TABLE OF CONTENTS

INTRODUCTION

Philip Handler
President, National Academy of Sciences

Many years ago, although perhaps never stated explicitly, it appears to have been agreed that it is the role of government to protect the citizen from those aspects of his personal environment against which he cannot protect himself. In a sense, this was the reason for establishing police forces, fire departments, armies, and navies.

As technology increasingly pervaded our civilization, numerous and diverse regulatory agencies were created at federal, state, and municipal levels. These agencies, charged with a difficult, complex task, are part of the system in our society by which we oppose tensions, situations in which one element of society advances its proposal and another element contends with it. Out of the contention come decisions, hopefully in the public interest.

The subject of this first Academy Forum -- "How Safe is Safe? The Design of Policy on Drugs and Food Additives" -- is such a consideration. In discussions of this topic, the phrase "cost and risk-benefit analysis" occurs repeatedly. But this is really a facile phrase rather than a reference to a developed science or art. The ground rules for such analyses have not been spelled out, nor am I aware of an important decision outside the military which has really rested on what might be described as a formal, careful cost and risk-benefit analysis.

Two difficulties underlie this situation. First, rarely is it true that we have the information required to perform a persuasive cost and risk-benefit analysis. Usually when a matter of concern comes to public attention, and becomes the responsibility of an appropriate regulatory agency, it already carries a sense of urgency. Although the agency knows that it does not have enough information to make a decision with the certainty it would like to have, it cannot avoid the responsibility for decision. This is certainly true in regard to drugs and food additives, for which we are beset by the tyranny of a large number, 2×10^8, the population of the United States.

Suppose that by _safe_ we mean knowledge that an untoward incident is not likely to happen with a frequency of more than 10^{-6}. If the entire population were exposed, that would still result in 200 unfortunate accidents. Someone must decide whether that is an acceptable order of safety. Meanwhile, we must realize that to establish that untoward incidents will not occur with a frequency greater than 10^{-6} is a monumental task.

The toxicological literature is rich in descriptions of the physiological responses to a huge number of compounds at dosage levels high enough to assure such response. But it is understandably meager with respect to the lowest regions of dose-response curves -- and in most real-life situations those are the data required.

In addition to the enormity of the experimental problem, there is also the confusion which frequently reigns in such matters as they come to attention. Perhaps the best example of this problem is that of DDT. I have undergone the masochistic exercise of reading a considerable part of those hundreds of pages of testimony which were taken by the hearing examiner who "examined DDT" and then made his recommendations to the administrator of the Environmental Protection Agency. I say "masochistic" quite deliberately. Two-thirds of the so-called "scientific evidence" that I read could not have found acceptance by the editorial board of a reputable scientific journal.

The situation was summed up, I thought, in the remarkable words of the administrator of EPA in the decision statement in which DDT was effectively banned for most purposes. As close as I can recall it, he said "DDT constitutes an unquantifiable hazard of uncertain nature." As a basis for decision making I find that somewhat less than persuasive. I am not disagreeing with the decision itself, please understand. It is the basis for decision making, the inadequacy of the data, which I found so very troublesome. I still do. The burden on the scientific community, it seems to me, is to provide adequate bases for such decisions in the future.

The second difficulty lies in the calculus. How does one calculate a cost or risk-benefit analysis? It is fairly easy when the units on both sides of an equation are stated in the same dimensions. When a business corporation is deciding what to do with the funds available for investment it invests dollars, and what it examines are the rates of return, in dollars, in alternate situations; decision making then is fairly simple.

There are other situations where there are equivalent terms on both sides of the equation. For example, if we wish to know whether a given, purportedly life-saving, drug is acceptable for use in a fatal disease, and if the data at hand indicate that the use of that drug may kill 10 people for each 1,000 that it would cure, the odds are 100 to 1 in favor of a random patient. I would not have much trouble with such a decision.

However, in many cases the dimensions on the two sides of the equation are non-equivalent, particularly in environmental and consumer matters, with dollars on one side and, on the other, human lives or less quantifiable social amenities. In such situations, there is no escape from the need, somehow, to equate dollars and lives, to agree to the dollar value of an average human life in the population at risk. For example, automobiles have been killing more than 50,000 people per year on the highways and maiming five times that number. Suppose we knew how to reduce that carnage by half; what then is the magnitude of the expenditure that we would be willing to accept annually to accomplish that goal? There are several approaches to such calculations; each leaves one uncomfortable for one or another reason. But until we settle that question, we will be unable to engage in logical decision making in many instances.

In other instances, however, one can imagine value judgments that override seemingly rational "dollar considerations". For example, I do not know the dollar cost to the nation of drug abuse. But we find drug abuse so repugnant that our willingness to combat it may well exceed the "dollar value" of the lives destroyed by drugs. We would undoubtedly spend a great deal if only we knew what to do usefully. Similarly, in some of the instances discussed in this Forum, non-dollar value judgments take over. All cost and risk-benefit analyses entail a greater or lesser degree of social, political, or ethical judgment. To the extent that they do, every layman is at least as well qualified as a scientist to participate in the decision making process.

Generally, in regard to drugs and food additives, there are a few simple ground rules on which we can probably agree. One is that large benefits certainly justify larger risks than small benefits, and that where there is no benefit, no risk is acceptable if it can be avoided. One can imagine instances in which value judgments would take over so that this rule would be violated; but it seems a reasonable guideline for behavior. And, taken by and large, this is the way we have behaved.

It is more difficult to document that this has indeed been the pattern of decision making for compounds at the margin of decision making. The decision with respect to cyclamates certainly was not couched in those terms. The benefit side of the equation was never estimated or considered, in part because of the difficult task of comparing incommensurables, in part for lack of data concerning risk or benefit in real life situations. Hence, a relatively uninformed value judgment took over.

Also, we must acknowledge the difference between publicly inflicted and privately accepted risks, namely those risks which one undertakes voluntarily and those which cannot be avoided because the rest of society imposes them upon us. In a general way, most of us will voluntarily accept risks about two orders of magnitude greater than we will accept when the rest of the society imposes them.

Returning to the statement I made earlier, regulatory agencies will repeatedly be confronted with the need for decision making with an insufficiency of data. At such times, they have no choice; they must then err on the side of conservatism when protection of public health is involved. That is their role in our society, the only choice that is before them. The fact that they cannot always justify those actions fully will rest on that philosophy; it is, in fact, their very business.

I am pleased with the choice of subject for the first Academy Forum, the safety of drugs and food additives. It is a problem which is much in the press, although the stories, in my view, tend to be somewhat one-sided. The National Academy of Sciences has been subject to some criticism for its role in this process on several occasions. In retrospect, I believe that each of the reports in question was technically sound, but there may be room for honest disagreement based on the value judgments I have already noted.

My own concern with the subject is of long standing. When I went to North Carolina in 1938, pellagra was the leading cause of death in eight southeastern states. Every spring virtually all the beds in every hospital in the South filled up with pellagrins, and so did every available bed in every mental institution. It was a dreadful situation.

Not long before I went there it had been found that nicotinic acid is a vitamin, and pellagra was deemed to be a vitamin deficiency disease. Certainly administration of nicotinic acid could cure pellagra. My own research was concerned with the physiological role of nicotinic acid and the physiological consequences of deficiency.

At the time, several of us developed the notion that the most effective way to get at pellagra as a problem in public health was not to await revitalization of the economy of the South, nor for doctors to tour the countryside with hypodermics full of nicotinic acid. The predictably effective preventive would be to add nicotinic acid to cornmeal, the staple of the pellagra-producing diet. We had already fortified commercial wheat flour with thiamine by that time. So several of us toured the South, trying to talk state legislators into introducing legislation which would make it mandatory to fortify corn flour with nicotinic acid.

The episode of which I am fondest happened one day before a committee of the North Carolina legislature. There was no air conditioning, and the committee room was extraordinarily hot. The chairman of the committee was a caricature of a southern legislator, decidedly obese, and fanning himself while dripping perspiration. I went through my little song and dance explaining that pellagra was a deficiency disease due both to lack of nicotinic acid and the fact that cornmeal has a poorly understood but positive role in the etiology. All pellagrins, everywhere in the world, eat corn, and if we were to fortify corn flour with nicotinic acid the disease could be prevented.

When I finished, the chairman glared at me and said, "Young man, don't you think that if the good Lord intended for corn to have that nicotinic acid he would have put it there? Is man really wiser than the good Lord?"

I was twenty-three years old -- and stunned. After a long silence, I managed to say, "Why no, sir. The good Lord performed a miracle. Each time you put one of those corn seeds in the ground and water it, in due course you get a perfect corn plant. That is what the Lord intended. It was fools like me and you who decided to eat those corn seeds instead."

During a prolonged hush, I watched a play of emotions across his face, and then he burst out in a great guffaw. That legislature passed the law the next day. Pellagra disappeared within two years, in no small part because of the fortification program.

I tell this story today because it did not occur to me until some time thereafter that I had no idea whether there might be any ill effects from putting nicotinic acid into the corn. When I then fed to some dogs the standard black-tongue producing diet but containing cornmeal fortified with nicotinic acid, nothing happened, fortunately.

Two years following that, for quite different reasons, I fed nicotin-amide, the form in which the vitamin occurs in coenzymes, to young rats at various levels in the diet. At about 0.3 percent of the diet, their growth was markedly impaired; they developed large, fatty livers which went on to become cirrhotic. Had I done that experiment first, I would never have had the courage to sell a program for the fortification of cornmeal with nicotinic acid. Nor am I certain what the Food and Drug Administration would have done had the program been challenged. What would that agency do today?

That story involves various of the considerations to be explored in this Forum: the notion that the living organisms found in nature are in some way sanctified as particularly appropriate for man to eat; the problem of the difference between the safe and the dangerous levels of a given substance, in this case one which is stated to be a vitamin. Note that the margin of safety is less than the usual factor of 100 which some of our committees advocate, that is, the margin between the nutritional requirement of these animals and the amount that will give them fatty livers. Similarly, with respect to Vitamin A and Vitamin D, the margin between the optimal dose and the dangerous dose is smaller than would be permitted for a food additive. Is that a problem with which we must concern ourselves?

Again, it must be done by some evaluation of the relative risks and benefits, but by what calculus?

Patently, I bring a thirty-year-old interest to our subject. The problems surrounding it recently have been paraded before us on the front pages, in scientific meetings, and have been in the courts for some years. All of us are aware that there has been a great deal of heat in these discussions. One purpose of this Forum is to see whether, more importantly, any light has been shed.

ACADEMY FORUM: Part I

DANIEL E. KOSHLAND, JR.
        CHAIRMAN

DANIEL E. KOSHLAND, JR.: This Academy Forum will try to illuminate some of the frequently dark areas between objective scientific fact and subjective societal values. Its purpose is not to make specific decisions, but rather to examine the bases on which the design of policy on drugs and food additives is constructed. John Hogness and I will act somewhat as marshals as we attempt to keep the discussion focused on evaluations of policy and on methods which will allow us to quantify risk-benefit analysis.

We have tried to assemble a variety of viewpoints in our speakers, discussants, and audience. This group is a great encouragement to us, for it represents science, government, policy makers, ordinary citizens, consumers, just the kind of assembly we had hoped for. Such a gathering has its liabilities, however. If everyone is to have a chance to participate, it will be necessary to dispense with the usual amenities and protocols. One which I regret deeply is an enumeration of all the people who have contributed so vitally to developing the Forum. Their names and roles are listed in the program. I urge you to consult those lists, for they represent the distillation of hours of effort and years of wisdom. I also will dispense with a review of the biographical data on our participants. That also is presented in your program and will assure you of their extensive capabilities and experience. It thus remains my pleasure to introduce our first two speakers.

James S. Turner is a lawyer and author who has invested much of his seemingly endless supply of energy in furthering consumer affairs. He is founder and co-director of Consumer Action for Improved Food and Drugs. His viewpoint should introduce some new questions for consideration.

W. Clarke Wescoe is vice chairman of the Board of Sterling Drug Company and president of the Winthrop Laboratories Division. Prior to assuming his present duties in industry, Dr. Wescoe was chancellor of the University of Kansas. He brings a wide and varied experience to his viewpoint of the producer.

A Consumer's Viewpoint

James S. Turner

"How safe is safe?" is a misleading question for a conference on the design of policy on drugs and food additives. It implies the quest for an objective,
scientific, if you will, standard of safety acceptable to all interested in the
issue being considered. Unfortunately, in the real world today's acceptable
standard of safety may be more or less acceptable than yesterday's or tomorrow's.

In addressing the problem of nuclear reactor safety, Dr. Alvin Weinberg,
director of the Oak Ridge National Laboratory, puts the matter more precisely
when he asks, "How safe is safe enough?" That is the question underlying the
design of policy on drugs and food additives. It is not primarily a question
for scientists; it is a policy question.

Dr. Weinberg spelled out the distinction effectively when he spoke at the
dedication of the Paul B. Johnson Science Tower at the University of Southern
Mississippi in January 1972:

> Many of the issues that arise in the course of the interaction
> between science or technology and society -- e.g., the deleterious
> side effects of technology, or the attempts to deal with social prob-
> lems through the procedures of science -- hang on the answers to ques-
> tions which can be asked of science and yet which cannot be answered
> by science. I propose the term trans-scientific for these questions
> since, though they are, epistemologically speaking, questions of fact
> and can be stated in the language of science, they are unanswerable
> by science; they transcend science. Insofar as public policy depends
> on trans-scientific rather than scientific issues, the role of the
> scientist in contributing to the promulgation of such policy must be
> different than is his role when the issues can be unambiguously an-
> swered by science.

In conclusion Dr. Weinberg states:

> When what we [scientists] do transcends science and when it im-
> pinges on the public, we have no choice but to welcome the public --
> even encourage the public -- to participate in the debate. Scientists

have no monopoly on wisdom where this kind of trans-science is involved; they shall have to accommodate to the will of the public
and its representatives.

Safety as it has come to be used within the context of the food and drug

laws and the complex of regulations supporting them is a trans-scientific problem.

Under current laws a substance can be found safe only if it has passed through

three phases of consideration. The nature of the safety problem may be better

understood if it is examined within this context.

First is the objective, scientific determination of the discernible effects

involved in the chemical's use. This determination is the responsibility of

scientists.

Second is the judgment about which of these effects is a risk and which is

a benefit. This judgment is ultimately made by the public, acting through its

representatives and spokesmen or as individuals, but acting with a high degree of

guidance from scientists, physicians, or other trained professionals.

Third is the decision that the agreed upon benefits of a given chemical ex-

ceed its agreed upon risks. This is a public, not a scientific, decision, made

in public forums in which scientists act as equal, though in some cases better

informed, participants with other segments of the public.

A safe chemical is one that has passed through all three phases satisfactorily.

Its effects are known and agreed upon with some certainty by qualified scientists.

The benefits and risks of the chemical have been sorted out accurately to the

general satisfaction of the society. The society then has decided that the bene-

fits of the use of the chemical in the way permitted outweigh its risks.

Unfortunately, this is not the way the determinations of chemical safety

always work. Certain dramatic regulatory decisions during the past twenty years

illustrate why the public increasingly doubts industrial, regulatory, and scientific assertions that the food and drug supplies are safe enough. The approval and then the subsequent banning of cyclamate, including the unnecessary references to the Delaney anti-cancer clause, illustrate the problems that occur when scientists cannot agree on the potential effects of a given chemical, but regulators act as if they do. The premature approval of the Salk polio vaccine and the subsequent 260 cases of vaccine-associated polio, 10 of which resulted in death, delineate the tragedy that can result when risks and benefits are improperly identified or weighed. The negligent release of certain lots of Sabin Type III oral polio vaccine and subsequent findings against the government for that action suggest that the public is going to hold science and scientists to an increasing degree of responsibility for their decisions. Each of these events has a lesson which can be helpful in determining how safe is safe enough.

In 1963, the Division of Biologic Standards (DBS) of the National Institutes of Health, then the nation's vaccine regulators, approved certain lots of Sabin Type III polio vaccine for use in a Philadelphia mass-immunization campaign. A Philadelphia housewife, who was forty-one years old at the time, took a dose of one of the lots and contracted polio from the vaccine. She became a permanent quadriplegic.

After reviewing the case during seven years of legal proceedings, the federal district court in Philadelphia ruled that the vaccine lots had been released negligently by the DBS. It awarded damages of over $1 million to the injured party. Evidence showed that government scientists responsible for protecting the public had kept shoddy, incomplete, or misleading records about vaccine safety. It showed that the statistical methods used to evaluate test findings were poorly constructed -- so much so, in fact, that the presiding judge pointed to them as "...a perfect example of the old...chestnut, 'garbage in, garbage out'."

Evidence introduced into the record suggested that when the mass-inoculation campaign was in the planning stages the Public Health Service's ad hoc polio advisory committee voted six to four to include a warning against the use of the Sabin Type III oral vaccine by adults. Subsequently the committee was informed by the manufacturer that "...the company must give serious consideration to the possibility that the Type III vaccine will have to be withdrawn from commercial sale...if labeling precautions cannot be written with adequate safeguards that will not deter its sale...." Following this statement by the company the committee reversed itself, removing the warning about adults.

A careful examination of the regulatory records on Sabin polio vaccine revealed a nightmare of improper, mistaken, or negligent action -- including a total lack of familiarity with the laws and regulations governing vaccine control on the part of the responsible officials -- all taken in the name of and on behalf of science. The surprising reaction of officials faced with the responsibility for the $1 million judgment was to suggest that the regulations be changed so that their actions would become legal.

When the safety problem is viewed in this context the issues related to benefit and risk become less esoteric, abstract, and philosophical. The problem becomes a practical one. Mechanisms must be designed to ensure that the individuals charged with applying the available scientific knowledge to regulatory decisions have a proper sense of responsibility and a clear knowledge that they will be held accountable for their mistakes, as well as rewarded for their contributions. Until these mechanisms are developed, the public sense that the chemical environment is not safe enough will continue to grow. Unless the world of scientific decision making on behalf of the public is opened to public scrutiny and evaluation, more and more policy restraints will be placed on the granting of responsibility to scientists. Alvin Weinberg puts the situation bluntly: "The republic of science can be destroyed more surely by withdrawal of public support for science than by intrusion of the public into its workings."

The government's problem with certain lots of Sabin vaccine suggests how skeptical the public, through its trans-scientific institutions, is becoming of so-called scientific discretion. However, the Salk vaccine incident introduces another dimension. It suggests that the real safety problem involves not only a better weighing of benefits and risks, but the development of a better identification of benefits and risks.

The 260 victims of polio contracted from the Salk vaccine have often been the centerpiece in a number of theoretical discussions about risk-benefit. The trade-off is always between the number injured by the vaccine versus the number who would have been injured if the vaccine had not been used. H. V. Wyatt, in his article appearing in the January 26, 1973, issue of Nature, "Is Polio a Model for Consumer Research?," sums it up: "The situation, although regrettable, was certainly less severe than it might have been if the vaccine had not been used."

This is a comforting thought. But it lets science and the regulatory officials responsible for applying it off the hook too easily. If they had done their job properly the full benefit of the vaccine could have been had without the 260 casualties. This certainly would have been better than what occurred.

Dr. James Shannon said, in a 1966 address to the Oklahoma Frontiers of Science Foundation, that the Salk vaccine represented a scientific error. "...the decision of the Foundation [National Foundation for Infantile Paralysis] to throw its resources behind the development of an inactivated vaccine markedly increased the difficulties and greatly protracted the time required to develop the generally accepted polio vaccine we have today." The New York Times article reporting that speech states that "Dr. Shannon felt the 'error' of the National Foundation derived in part from the secrecy of its operations, which limited the input of external ideas."

Dr. Shannon's view is a retrospective one. It can be considered in future situations, but reasonable men could have disagreed about the choices when they were made in 1955. It is more difficult to accept the fact that in 1955 the bench scientists at the Division of Biologic Standards responsible for evaluating the safety of Salk vaccine refused free doses for their children. They did so because more than six months before the beginning of the Salk mass-immunization program three monkeys came down with what appeared to be a paralysis caused by the vaccine. This warning did not cause those responsible for the program to search out a potential problem. Six months later, when the first five vaccine-related cases of polio were detected, a massive crisis program was undertaken to find and correct the problem. Within thirty days the reason for live polio contamination of the vaccine had been discovered, corrected, and the vaccine was back on the market.

In a program as important, sensitive, and dramatic as the Salk mass-immunization campaign, three sick monkeys should have been an effective early warning of the problems to come. That they were not suggests important weaknesses in the system for identifying risks and benefits which must be corrected before the weighing of benefits and risks can be seriously undertaken.

The manipulation of science to make risks appear more acceptable, illustrated by the Philadelphia Sabin case, and the failure of science to detect warnings, as in the Salk case, feed public skepticism about claims that all is well with food and drugs. This skepticism, shared by a good number of scientists, underlies the strong support for the Delaney anti-cancer clause of the food and drug law, which prohibits the use in human foods of any chemical which has caused cancer when ingested by man or animal.

In October of 1969, the Secretary of Health, Education, and Welfare removed cyclamate from the list of food chemicals generally recognized as safe, better known as the GRAS list. He removed the chemical not because scientists agreed that it was unsafe, but because it could no longer be said that scientists agreed that it was safe. A number of observations contributed to this doubt concerning cyclamate. It produced a human metabolite which caused genetic damage in rats. It and the metabolite caused teratogenic damage in chickens. It bound itself to plasma, thus inhibiting drug delivery to the body. It inhibited the effect of Vitamin K. It had caused some unreported cancerous tumors in 1950 FDA tests. When combined with saccharin, it had caused cancer in rats.

For apparently political reasons the Secretary made unnecessary references to the Delaney anti-cancer clause to justify removal of the chemical from the GRAS list. The clause reads as follows: "Provided, That no additive shall be deemed to be safe if it is found to induce cancer when ingested by man or animal, or if it is found, after tests which are appropriate for the evaluation of the safety of food additives, to induce cancer in man or animal...."

It was unnecessary even to refer to the clause in banning cyclamate because once safety became a question, the chemical could not be used unless it had been tested and shown to be safe. This meant that its effects had to be demonstrated, that its benefits and risks had to be sorted out and then weighed. If qualified scientists had found during this period that the chemical did cause cancer when ingested by man or animal, then the Delaney clause could have been invoked. The previously made public determination that the potential risk of including a cancer-causing chemical in the food supply outweighs any benefits that the chemical might have would then have controlled the situation. If this procedure, as outlined in the law, had been followed, the importance of the Delaney clause could have been more accurately assessed and appreciated. Instead, the premature reference to the clause led to a widespread misunderstanding of the purpose and principle underlying it.

The principle of the Delaney clause is that weighing of benefits and risks is not a purely scientific question; it is a policy question that requires an informed public decision. The principle of the Delaney clause is that the weighing of benefits and risks is not the sole province of a regulatory agency or its scientific advisors. The Delaney clause applies this principle to those chemicals which cause cancer when ingested by man or animal. It does this on the advice of a large segment of the scientific community which argues that the effects of even traces of a cancer-causing substance cannot be predicted. Relying on this advice the public had adopted the policy that no benefit is worth the possible hazard of adding a cancer-causing chemical to the food supply. The clause rests on scientific discretion. Scientists -- and scientists alone -- make the determination that an ingested chemical has caused cancer. The clause rests on the accepted operating principle that there is some relationship between the effects of the chemical on animals and its effects on man. This is the principle that allows drugs and food additives to be shown safe and to be marketed. The clause avoids the demand of absolute safety. Instead it says that in relation to the cancer risk the food supply will be safe enough only if no additional cancer-causing chemicals are added to it.

The Delaney clause can certainly be improved, but the central principle on which it rests must be kept intact. Safety is a policy question which demands the weighing of properly identified risks and benefits by the public. It is not an objective, scientific determination. The weighing mechanism can be improved, but improvement will not be accomplished by giving regulatory authorities more bureaucratic discretion. The Delaney clause, unlike any other section of the Food, Drug, and Cosmetic Act, recognizes and is premised upon the limitations of science.

The Food Safety Panel of the 1969 White House Conference on Food, Nutrition, and Health stated the limitation on proving food chemical safety. The panel said, "It is not possible to determine with absolute certainty the safety of the ever-increasing number of chemicals added to or present in our foods." As a member of the panel I concurred with that statement. It appeared to me to be a warning. Since science could never be sure of a chemical's safety, it seemed obvious that as a matter of policy we should be cautious in allowing the use of chemicals in food. Unfortunately, many individuals both inside and outside of science took this statement to mean the opposite. Since safety cannot ever be proven conclusively, they argued, we ought to be cautious in restricting the use of chemicals. It is this attitude against which public sentiment is reacting.

Increasingly scientific evidence relates various chemicals to serious problems of human health. Responsible scientists have suggested that some chemicals may contribute to the development of certain kinds of mental retardation, 95 percent of which is of unknown origin. A large portion of the cancer research community spends its time evaluating the capability of various chemicals to cause cancer, although the cause is yet to be found. Some geneticists suggest that chemicals used in foods and drugs might play an important role in causing much of the society's genetic and mutagenic damage. For example, 20 to 30 percent of American pregnancies end in spontaneous abortion, stillbirth, or deformity.

Scientific research has identified a number of serious health problems for which the causes are at best elusive. It has also generated enough evidence to suggest a possible relationship between these disease conditions and the growing use of a number of chemicals in the drug and food supply. Diseases of unknown origin and chemicals with suspicious side effects combine to raise questions of drug and food additive safety and policy to a high level of public concern.

Increasingly pointed public questions are being raised about assumptions underlying chemical regulation. Dr. Jacqueline Verrett and Jean Carper, both of whom played an important role in the cyclamate ban, ask these in their book to be published in 1974 by Simon & Schuster, Eating Can Be Hazardous to Your Health:

> When industry tosses around the term benefit-risk, what do they mean? Do they mean consumer health benefits weighed against consumer health risks? Or consumer economic benefit against consumer health risk? Or some kind of consumer social benefit, such as time saving, against consumer health risk? Or, on the other hand, do they mean industry economic benefit against consumer health risk?

My experience is that industry means all of these. This fact, too, raises the level of public concern about drug and food additive safety and policy.

The point of all this is that the safety of drugs and food additives as a function of the weighing of benefits and risks is not what the public concern is all about. The real problem is twofold. The effects of chemicals in food and drugs have not yet been determined satisfactorily. No generally accepted definition of benefits and risks has been agreed upon. It is on these two problems that from the consumer's point of view the attention of science should be focused.

A Producer's Viewpoint

W. Clarke Wescoe, M.D.

It is not a particularly prevailing attitude of the times for one designated a producer to be invited to participate prominently in a program directed
toward a discussion of public policy. To many it appears that the term producer
has achieved a pejorative meaning in our society. Today it is considered almost
improper to produce. To be socially respectable one has only to consume.

The very format of this Forum may indicate to some that in the matter of
safety relating to food additives and medicinal products there are necessarily
divergent viewpoints among those who make, those who use, those who are concerned
with biological science, and those who are charged with the responsibility to
administer the laws. I choose to think quite the opposite is true. In this, as
in many other areas, it is not a matter of we and they, us and them, the good
guys and the bad guys. It is not a matter of conflicting interests, of adversary relationships. Rather it is a collective matter of trying to reach a common
goal: the provision of calculable benefit to man with as little attendant risk
as possible.

In a civilized society there is no more important goal. In pursuit of that
goal we are all as one. There is no place for emotional catchwords. There are no
reasons for artificial designations. There should be no acceptance of superficial
stereotypes. Obviously, I am not only a producer; I am a consumer as well. In each
of those stances I am caught up constantly in the assessment of benefits and risks.
I choose to believe that as a producer I am the most deeply "concerned," to use
the vernacular of the day. I choose to believe that as a producer I am most

likely to assess the circumstances most carefully, for I must live with the assessments that are made in relation to the products with which I am associated. To be a producer is to conduct one's affairs all day so that one can sleep easily all through the night.

We live in a "no-fault," "no-risk," "all-safe" society. The no-fault concept deals primarily with individuals. The no-risk, all-safe concepts are associated primarily with products. We strive in our preoccupation with those concepts for a circumstance that man has never enjoyed and for a utopian existence most probably beyond his reach. Man has always been at risk in his world, and he always will be. As one risk has been removed, another sometimes unpredicted risk inevitably has been added.

Our very concern today is an example of that historic repetition. Disease has been suppressed. Contagion has been conquered. Nutrition has been improved. However, the very agents that produced advances once hailed as miracles are now called into question. Society must continue to live with risks, as it always has. The risks must be calculated, assessed and then, hopefully, controlled as a result of balanced, unemotional discussion in the absence of fanaticism, hysteria, and hyperbole. Public policy should derive from reason, objectivity, and scientific evaluation of pertinent data. However, balanced, unemotional discussion has always been difficult to obtain.

I know of no particular groups who have achieved this goal in terms of the absolute. Objectivity is obviously at risk in any controversy. Consequently, in striving for objectivity it is necessary to scrutinize carefully the circumstances that may compromise it. It is just this necessity that brings us together to discuss the safety of food additives and medicines.

No discussion of this nature can be held without mentioning the forty-nine

words that have come to be known as the Delaney clause: "Provided, That no additive shall be deemed to be safe if it is found to induce cancer when ingested by
man or animal, or if it is found, after tests which are appropriate for the evaluation of the safety of food additives, to induce cancer in man or animal...."

Herein, special legislation deals in singular, unique fashion with the mani-
festation of a single chemical toxicity. I discuss it with considerable trepida-
tion, for as Professor Arthur Bestor has written in his article appearing in the
October 1972 issue of Encounter: "Tolerance of opposing views is conceded to be
a fine thing, generally speaking, where routine matters only are involved. But
on certain issues one position seems so incontrovertibly right and the other so
infernally wrong that to be tolerant is to become the accomplice of wickedness."

I am one of those trained in the biological sciences who believes that biology is never a matter of absolutes, that all biologic phenomena must be expressed
as possibilities rather than as absolutes. In that belief I am confirmed by numbers of prominent scientists. Beyond that, out of my training as a pharmacologist, I consider the matter of dose-response to be fundamental. In that consideration I am even joined by eminent scientists who are not pharmacologists. For
instance, Dr. John Higginson, director of the International Agency for Research
on Cancer, has said that knowledge of concentrations at which a substance becomes
carcinogenic may allow it to be used in lower concentrations. Here is a leading
pathologist who invokes the principle of dose-response.

The words of the Delaney clause allow no consideration of dose-response as
I read them. I am aware that there are others who believe that the principle of
zero tolerance must be accepted for any substance shown in any concentration to
be carcinogenic in animals. In their thinking, a safe level for man cannot be
established for agents shown in any species to be carcinogenic. They do, however,

recognize as a realistic notion the concept of, as they call it, "socially acceptable risk." That notion is foreclosed by the clause. The experimental feeding of
high concentrations of a particular substance as a caricature of what man conceivably could ingest is toxicologically naïve and also ignores basic pharmacologic
principles. It is possible with high concentrations to overload the system of elimination by which a substance normally would be handled. Under those circumstances
alternative pathways of elimination can be called into play or the substance can
accumulate in an abnormal way. The alternate (unreal) pathway or the accumulation
itself could be the factor implicated in the end result observed. An experiment
of this nature bears little relationship to reality.

Those who do not believe in a no-effect level essentially discard the all-
embracing ground rules of statistical biology which were scientifically established
by Sir Ronald Fisher and which have been validated repeatedly in every other
sphere of science. Beyond that they tend to ignore the difficulties involved in
extrapolating animal data in a meaningful way to man.

Most recently the Delaney clause was called into play when a prohibition was
placed necessarily on the use of diethylstilbestrol (DES) as a feed additive for
cattle. That particular decision was a triumph of superior, sophisticated analytical technique that permitted the measurement of 120 parts per trillion of DES
in cattle liver, not, as I read it, in the musculature of the cattle.

Inevitably, as we develop highly sophisticated techniques, we shall begin to
discover the presence in tissues of more and more substances in lesser and lesser
amounts. This possibility has now become apparent to perceptive laymen, as witness the editorial from the New York Times of April 30, 1973, entitled "Policy
on Infinitesimals." A portion of that editorial reads:

> Such sensitivity in measuring infinitesimal quantities is a res-
> pectable scientific feat, but how meaningful is it as a guide to the
> public? Is there a significant -- even an appreciable -- risk of
> anyone getting cancer from eating meat containing so tiny a quantity
> of DES? How does the "risk" the FDA has moved against compare with
> the risk of breathing normal polluted air in Manhattan or downtown
> Washington, D.C. -- or with the risk of having a chest X-ray or smoking
> a single cigarette?
>
> The point is that the Delaney amendment is an all or nothing affair,
> and presumably would have applied if the analytical equipment had found
> only one thousandth of a trillionth part of DES. This sounds more like
> fanaticism than intelligent public policy. Would not Congress be well
> advised to consult the scientists on what meaning, if any, the law
> should give to infinitesimal quantities?

This editorial expresses the difficulties inherent in the legislative prescrip-

tion of absolutes relative to biological systems.

All that we discuss of safety must, of course, be examined from the stand-

point of evaluating the magnitude of the possible risk involved in comparison

with the extent of the benefit desired.

In respect of food additives of certain sorts, such as flavors and colors,

the benefit derived from a societal standpoint may be so small as to obviate the

consideration of exposure to any risk, no matter how small. I must remark, how-

ever, that I could not conceive that any human has ever been exposed to a risk of

cancer because he ate meat stamped by governmental inspectors with FD&C Violet No.

1. In respect of other food additives, such as those used for purposes of preser-

vation and those used for special dietary purposes, the benefit derived may be

significant enough to allow the consideration of a certain degree of assessable

risk at a low level.

I presume there is no time available to deal at length with the matter about

which present legislation is silent -- the tumorigenic or carcinogenic properties

of natural foods. Just for the sake of completeness we should not fail to men-

tion the long years and the many generations that have witnessed the consumption of cabbage, spinach, and brussels sprouts, all of which are goitrogenic if fed to animals in high enough quantities, and the more recent detection of the known carcinogens, aflatoxin and safrole, in natural products that are widely ingested.

At least in respect of these natural foods we have epidemiologic and geographic studies available to us. In respect of food additives the case is more complex. Food additives become widely distributed in random fashion. Their presence is often unknown or unsuspected in many foods and beverages. The very ubiquitous nature of their use requires a close assessment of their possible risks. It requires, as well, careful analysis of their toxicologic properties. The enactment of legislation in 1958 relative to food additives was a necessary and important step despite the fact that the forty-nine words of the Delaney clause could have, in the opinion of some of us, been better written in a different way.

In respect of drugs -- and I prefer to call them medicines -- we are faced with considerations of a different order. Here we talk about products designed to produce great benefit. We talk necessarily, however, of products that carry an inherent risk, for a drug, by its very nature, cannot be totally safe for everyone. The basic tenet of pharmacology is that any drug action is a toxicity, even the desired action, simply because in that action some cellular process is modified. Although in these desirable toxic actions we can tell with reasonable certainty the parameters of the risk, we cannot provide a certificate of safety. Most scientists, but few of the general public, understand this principle relating to medicines. René Dubos perhaps put it most clearly when he spoke generally of technological innovation: "Willingness to take risks is a condition of biological success....Excessive concern with safety is often incompatible with economic growth....To demand a certified verdict of safety before accepting a new technological innovation would clearly result in paralysis of progress."

The public has learned to live willingly with risk in many spheres of activity and, it should be noted, without recognizing that in doing so they have calculated an acceptable benefit-risk ratio for themselves. People drive motor cars despite the appalling death toll on our highways. They smoke although they have been warned of the dangers to health involved with it. They engage in dangerous recreation without a second thought. They submit to surgery oblivious to its morbidity and mortality rate. Regrettably, the public is not attuned to the same evaluation of benefit-risk as it relates to medicines and science. The public requires education in this area, the sort of education that this Forum may provide and the sort that could be provided by the talented efforts of the journalists who are present.

There is perhaps no other group of products so well regulated and so carefully controlled as are medicines in this country. In this field the producer has no conflict of interest with the consumer; neither does he have conflict with true science or with equitable regulation. Medicines differ from food additives and environmental chemicals in significant ways. They are designed from the beginning of chemical synthesis to achieve a benefit for man--improvement of health, alleviation of symptoms, cure of disease. Exposure to them is limited in terms of population and duration of use. They are administered in a controlled manner and in a dosage form that is recommended after exhaustive investigation. They are taken under the direction of a professional person who by reason of education and experience can decide whether obvious advantages justify an assessable risk. Because of background information available from years of intensive and expensive efforts in pharmaceutical research, carried out in industrial, academic, and governmental laboratories, there are well-defined tests for activity, efficacy, and safety available to us.

Over the years animal models have been developed. Sophisticated analytical techniques have been devised. Yet despite all the collected information, all the facts we can learn from laboratory studies and the undoubted intellectual attractiveness of studying reactions to medicines in animals, laboratory investigation in animals still remains an attractive hypothesis.

No animal, including the subhuman primate, is entirely and predictably like man. Differences in metabolic fate, differences in sensitivities, differences in immune mechanisms separate man from laboratory animals. For many differences there are no known short-term predictive tests. The truth is that absolute safety cannot be guaranteed despite years of intensive laboratory investigation. The final truth is that for medicines the ultimate test is careful evaluation and experience in man.

As man differs from other animals, so humankind differs among itself. An infant is not a small adult. A pregnant woman is different from a non-pregnant one. Enzymatic systems differ in the various races of man, a fact that leads to differing tolerances to medicines. We are, each of us, genetically different from hundreds of millions of others. Man is not a homogeneous species. Because man is heterogeneous, unanticipated, and unpredictable, side reactions occasionally occur from medicines. Fortunately, many of these are subjective only. Most of them are limited in extent and reversible in action if the medicine is withdrawn or the dose altered. An unpredicted side reaction, usually an idiosyncrasy, rarely is life threatening.

Although laboratory and clinical investigations are carefully controlled, and the data from them subjected to intense scrutiny and statistical evaluation, the same is not true for adverse reaction reporting. Most adverse reaction reports are anecdotal in nature, poorly evaluated, and often the result of post hoc ergo propter hoc reasoning, neglectful of other variables. I have known examples,

for instance, of adverse-reaction reporting in which careful analysis of body

fluids failed to reveal the presence of the medicine presumably implicated, but

did reveal the presence of another medicine. Our mechanisms of surveillance of so-

called adverse reactions are neither scientific nor modernized.

The nature of biology, characterized by individual variations, has encouraged

the biological scientist to develop means for describing quantitatively the be-

havior of a larger system by the study of small samples. He relies upon these

well-established statistical methods of evaluation to ensure reproducibility. In

many circumstances a negative result is just as important as a positive one, but

there are those who will believe only if a positive result occurs. There are

those who are only concerned with the "heads" on the coin.

The decision to release a medicine for use in man has always been an agonizing

one for the producer and for the regulatory agency. The tendency exists always

to ask for more tests, to delay the decision, for a non-decision is easier to make

than a positive one. Different tests are required for different classes of medi-

cines. Careful guidelines are constantly evaluated, for unnecessary tests put

handcuffs on investigation and delay the introduction of medicines. The final

decision is always weighted with the ultimate consumer in mind. Public policy is

well established through the new drug application procedure.

Recently the question of carcinogenicity and mutagenicity in medicines has

been raised, in part related to an extension of the philosophy surrounding the

testing of food additives and environmental chemicals. Pharmaceutical manufac-

turers, regulatory personnel, and academic scientists have worked intensively and

cooperatively on this problem of high priority about which all have a sense of

urgency. There is general agreement that a normal mutation rate in man is unknown, that there is absence of concrete data to link mutagenesis with carcinogenesis, that the relevance of mutagenic testing in bacteria or yeasts is remote as a definitive test, that testing must be performed in mammalian species even though the relevance of such testing is not yet known. There is no suggestion at the present time of the need for rigid recommendations, and hopefully there will never be rigid ones legislated.

There is, however, a determination that the principles of pharmacology and toxicology will not be ignored in such testing. Testing in animals is fraught with variables -- purity of material administered, diet consumed, air pollutants, water purity, among others. Agreement is general that the differences in testing must apply for medicines that are taken only occasionally, medicines taken only for short terms, and medicines taken for prolonged periods. By heeding the principles of pharmacology, caricature experiments can be avoided. Appropriate attention must be paid to dose-response, to route of administration, to elimination pathways, and to duration of exposure. Here, incidentally, is an example of progress voluntarily achieved -- progress that removes the necessity for special legislation.

There is nothing, and logically so, of more concern to man than his health and those factors that affect it. That concern dictates the necessity for him to be educated fairly, with all sides of the question presented, and the concept of benefit-risk consistently explained. There is no reason for scare headlines or inflammatory statements created out of flimsy bases. When scientific meetings are held today and nothing real or evidential is found to be said, the reports should give those facts. No service is performed by reporting the likelihood of delayed, insidious effects about which nothing is known and which could not be measured, or by reporting the possibility of subtle damage, so subtle that it cannot be found. All of us are concerned with safety, and, I believe, the producer most of all. All of us are vigilant in searching out factors affecting safety. To the reasonable man vigilance means, as Arthur Bestor put it, "the precise identification of real dangers, not the hysterical shouting of 'Wolf,' 'Wolf,' when a mouse creeps out of the woodwork."

Complex issues demand careful and critical analysis. Reason, not emotion, should rule the day. The quiet voice is not easily heard in the din of chaotic clamor. All of us might well remember the words of Emerson in 1837, when he spoke to Phi Beta Kappa at Harvard on the responsibilities of the American scholar. We may not all be scholars, but we do search for truth. This is what Emerson said: "Let him not quit his belief that a popgun is a popgun, though the ancient and honorable of the earth affirm it to be the crack of doom."

DISCUSSION

KOSHLAND: It is quite clear from our first two speakers that men of good will can differ widely on complex matters. We will now turn to the discussion. Let us first hear from the Panel for Inquiry.

ROBERT McC. ADAMS: I have a question for Mr. Turner. He describes the central principle of the Delaney clause as being the weighing of properly identified risks and benefits by the public or the separation of the scientific determination from the public determination. It seems to me that the Delaney clause itself involves a central principle of zero tolerance, and in that sense limits the role of scientific determination to the effects under any circumstances. This is somewhat different than your earlier expression of the role of scientific determination being to assess the discernible effects, but presumably in that sense allowing for a concern for gradations of response.

JAMES S. TURNER: It seems to me that you are outlining the primary difficulty in the debate. The question is, To whom do you address your problem if you do not like what is happening? If you do not like the Delaney clause there are ways to proceed. What I am arguing is that a policy has been determined through policy making channels that there should be a zero tolerance. Zero tolerance is definitely there, and that was established on the basis of a great deal of scientific evaluation -- evaluation made up until 1970, when the last review of the Delaney clause by any governmental scientific body was undertaken. The evaluation wholeheartedly supported the clause, saying that we must retain the zero tolerance situation in the current state of cancer research or cancer knowledge.

Now, the issue remains a scientific one in the area of determining whether a chemical has or has not caused cancer. For example, I think a number of the problems which were identified by the producer spokesman indicated a concern about, for example, metabolic pathways or metabolic effects as identified in experiments. It is my reading of the Delaney clause, and the reading of many others who have studied it, that if scientists determined that a certain chemical did not cause cancer but that it was caused by something else in the system after a chemical was fed, the Delaney clause would not necessarily ban it. As a matter of fact it would not ban it. In other words, there is a great deal more scientific discretion in the clause than generally has been allowed.

Put another way, I think the argument about zero tolerance is off point. I think the real question is, Does the chemical cause cancer? I think that is a much more central scientific issue.

FRANKLIN A. LONG: Let me continue a bit with Mr. Turner along somewhat the same lines. I am a little uneasy about your particular use of the word _safe_. I am thinking of the early part of your statement when you were describing the various steps -- one, two, three -- that were taken in order to lead to a position of whether a drug or a chemical was safe. You stated that a safe chemical is one that has passed through all three phases satisfactorily.

I would think that the better term to use would be that it is an _approved_ chemical. It seems to me that the very notion of risk-benefit analysis means that indeed you will approve for certain uses and in certain doses and certain ways those materials that are not in another sense safe.

TURNER: I said "safe as used in the food and drug laws and the regulations underlying them." The important point that is central to this entire debate about the Delaney clause is that _safe_ has a policy meaning, that it means something as a public policy point. It also has come to have a meaning in terms of science, which you interpret in the scientific world as having more benefits than risks. But when we talk about a public policy issue, we talk about it as it is defined in law.

What is most intriguing to me is that the law, as it was originally drafted, defines safety as: "Any poisonous or deleterious substance added to any food except where such substance is required in the production thereof or cannot be avoided by good manufacturing practice shall be deemed to be unsafe for the purpose of the application of the clause." That is, anything that is poisonous or deleterious and is unnecessary shall be unsafe. Anything that is necessary will always be considered to be safe by the definition as it was drafted before the 1958 Act. We still have the hangover of some of that kind of thinking in the way the policy is applied.

What I was outlining was a policy of safety as it has come to be known within the food and drug law and regulations, and that is what I said. What you talk about when you talk about benefit-risk is the way safety has come to be discussed in scientific circles.

LONG: I must reject your last comment. I really was not talking about how we were looking at things in scientific circles at all. I was addressing the public policy decision, just exactly as you were. And it seems to me that one is frequently led into approving chemicals which in certain ways are not safe because their benefits in some situations outweigh their risks. The example that I will return to again, I am sure, is chloromycetin. In many ways we can honestly say that it is an unsafe material, and yet it also is an approved drug for specific use.

TURNER: But I also specifically addressed that point when I said, "Safe under the conditions permitted for use," and I specifically stated that. What I am trying to say -- and I really believe this is the central point to the whole discussion -- is that safety as a word and as a concept has two distinct parts. It has a scientific, hard research effect aspect, and it has a policy aspect. When we talk in public forums about safety we are talking about the mix of these aspects. So you can say that chloromycetin will have these bad effects, but it also will have these good effects, and then those are weighed. It is that weighing I was describing as the third step, when these mixed aspects come together to make a public policy position of safety in the food and drug area.

JOSHUA LEDERBERG: This is still to Mr. Turner. Is it a fair characterization of your discussion of Delaney that the legislation is a policy decision, that the risk of cancer has a value of minus infinity, and that therefore there could be no benefit that could conceivably outweigh the gravity of that risk as determined either by direct knowledge of the occurrence of cancer at any level in man or by extrapolation from experiments in animals?

KOSHLAND: I hate to ask you to repeat that question, but would you?

LEDERBERG: Is it a fair characterization that this is a policy determination that scientists should not quarrel with, that it is their job as technicians to determine whether or not a substance complies with the terms of the amendment but not to quarrel with the policy judgment that the value of cancer at any level is minus infinity?

TURNER: You just asked two questions. One was, "Is it my belief that the policy of the law clause is...?" And the other was, "Is it my belief that scientists should not quarrel with it?" Those are two distinct questions.

On the first point I think that yes, what you are saying is what the clause is. It is a policy statement of the kind that you have talked about. I also wish to make very clear that I did say -- and I am saying this not necessarily in response to your question, but in anticipation of some comments like the one that you made about scientists quarreling with it -- that I do believe that the clause can be improved. But I do believe that the principles underlying it are that it is a policy statement, and as such it sets out a role for scientists in their professional framework that is distinct from their role in policy evaluation framework. So I would say that while I think that what you are describing as the policy of the Delaney clause is in fact what the clause says, I have absolutely no problem with scientists arguing with it if they will argue within a public forum, saying the policy ought to be changed. But if they are coming in scientifically and saying that as a matter of science this is irrational, that is wrong. That is unscientific, and I think they make a mistake. I think they can come in and say it is a bad policy choice. Or if they have the data to prove conclusively, for example, that there is a dose relationship, then they can say, "Look, we were mistaken when this policy was made. Now it should be changed." But that is a very narrow kind of an attack. The broader discussions they have preferred are of the same kind a citizen might make.

LEDERBERG: I also have a question for Dr. Wescoe. Can you recite any example in which the Delaney clause has been invoked for infinitesimal levels of a potential carcinogen, and the case has been heard in a court to determine whether the defense of unreasonable application of the concept of infinitesimal has, in fact, been properly litigated?

W. CLARKE WESCOE: No. I do not know of any such instance.

LONG: I wanted to raise a general question which I guess is directed to Dr. Wescoe, but I am not sure. It is that a good deal of this discussion has rather implied that there is no time sequence to this decision making process. There is a phrase used in Dr. Wescoe's paper that the final decision is always weighed with the ultimate consumer in mind. I would have thought that a very important characteristic of all this policy making -- and I take it it is that -- is that it is going on continuously over time and that you do not just make a decision and settle it, but you make it and remake it. You make it on the basis of new evidence. I would think you would make it on the basis of a new drug, that is if you have done a risk-benefit analysis for one drug which may be somewhat hazardous but still seems essential. If a new drug is found for that same set of symptoms which is less hazardous, I should think you would have to rethink your previous decision, and I miss that sense of an ongoing set of decision making and policy making.

WESCOE: You have picked up something, of course, that is absolutely true, and one of those things that cannot be expressed when one is limited to exactly twenty-five minutes. Some clarifying, parenthetic facts are lost under those circumstances. Of course, the fact is that one is constantly weighing his decisions. From the standpoint of public policy and the Food, Drug, and Cosmetic Act there is now a greater weighing of the decisions by the producer and the regulatory agency together as experimental results are gradually assembled from all sources. Decisions are spread over a span of time.

PHILIP MORRISON: This question is addressed to the two speakers collectively.

I am puzzled by the language and the implied unassumed responsibility. It seems that the entire process is affected by this. It is of historical nature, but one talks about "generally regarded as safe." One talks about decisions about safety, but it seems all of the discussants generally agree that they are discussing quantitative questions of risk and benefit.

Why could there not be a more candid posture taken? Say this is a low-risk drug in a 1960 decision. In 1970 it remains there, a low-risk drug or additive. But it seems that the regulatory agencies and the statute assume more than man can really deliver in this interdependent world to assign safety. I do not know what effect it will have on the consumer. Cigarettes clearly are deemed rather unsafe, but their consumption does not much change. The sense of assuming risk on the part of the consumer is worthwhile in that context. What do you say about that? Would that be a big effect if we simply tried a much more candid approach toward the judgments that, in fact, the regulatory agencies and the producers are necessarily forced to make?

WESCOE: I do not think we can answer that one collectively. We will have to do it individually.

KOSHLAND: Each of you should answer. The legislative assistants in the audience can comment on the practicality of a bill being passed which says, "This protects the consumer to a 10^{-6} risk."

WESCOE: I think, in fact, Dr. Morrison, that there is a requirement for the public, who after all is the ultimate consumer, to be educated to the fact that there is nothing that is totally safe, not even some of the things we use every day and do not even think about. This water, for instance, for some people is

not totally safe unless the amount of it is measured very carefully. Since I
have not examined it microbiologically it might not even be safe for any of us
right now, but those are the risks we run. The words "generally recognized as safe"
were, I think, coined or used to make that apparent. It is a general recognition.
It is not an assumption of complete safety.

TURNER: I would answer you very quickly first, and then explain what I am saying.
I believe that what you have described is precisely what the Delaney clause is.
The problem with it, in the opinion of its critics, is that they do not like the
way the determination has come out as a policy determination. That is, the prin-
ciple of the Delaney clause is to eliminate the concept of safety from considera-
tion. I pointed this out in an article appearing in the October 1971 Vanderbilt
Law Review which defines the clause as a model for environmental protection law.
The clause is an effort to make a determination that we will allow something or
not allow something on the basis of some set of events. It speaks not of safety.
It is a proviso: Safety shall mean "Provided that ...." This is the principle which
I think you are talking for and which I believe is important. This is one discussion.

The next discussion in relation to the Delaney clause is whether the principle has been applied in a way which we like. That is a separate discussion. I
happen to think for the moment on the basis of what I can understand in the evaluations that are made for me that I like the way it has been defined. It may well
be that we as society would change that and set a principle statement which says
that we should have a residue of a certain amount or whatever. That may well be
what would occur. But I wanted to make a point about why in general I like the
Delaney clause as it now is.

Dr. Wescoe has pointed out clearly that food additives are distributed throughout the society widely and indiscriminately. It is virtually impossible for an individual now to make the kind of choice about buying a given food additive which may be involved with the Delaney kind of consideration that he makes when he buys cigarettes. That is, if I want to avoid a given substance about which there is controversy -- let us say FD&C Red No. 2, about which many people are concerned -- it is a virtual impossibility. I may be completely wrong in my determination that I wish to avoid it, but the risk is one that is decided by someone else for me. There is no question but that as a society we accept far less risks than we do as individuals. It may well be that even if we note on cans of soda pop containing FD&C Red No. 2 the presence of a chemical which many scientists believe has caused birth defects in animals, people would still buy it. If that is their choice, I would be happy with it. On the other hand, I might not buy it, and I would be happy with that as well.

KOSHLAND: Now may we have some questions from the Invited Discussants?

SAMUEL S. EPSTEIN: All the speakers have agreed on the existence of a wide range of divergent viewpoints on the basis of this calculus. I think one has to address oneself to two specific aspects of this problem.

The evaluation of the calculus demands that constraint-free data be analyzed and evaluated in constraint-free circumstances. This raises two questions. First, are the data on which decisions are now being made constraint free? Are they being analyzed in constraint-free circumstances? And second, what is the mechanism for introducing the alternative or the adversary viewpoint into the focus of the decision making process?

I think we are generally agreed that in a democratic society decisions are made, or should be made, in the open arena where alternative viewpoints are offered and where decisions are made on the basis of this. I would submit that the present system is calculated to produce data suffering from the maximum of constraints -- economically, politically and otherwise. Decisions on such data are made under circumstances of conflict of interest and in which the public interest has no formal representation whatsoever. Data generated under conditions of secrecy and conflict of interest -- and I would be happy to elaborate on this should a time arise -- are submitted to agencies and then evaluated and considered without balancing inputs on consumer public interest representatives. Therefore, I would like to ask Mr. Turner what suggestions he has for developing representation of the public interest and the scientific community, and for assigning legal representation of the public interest in the decision making process in existing regulatory agencies. Furthermore, I would like to know if he feels that the whole situation in existing regulatory agencies and their interface with the scientific and the technological community is adequate, or whether it is necessary to establish consumer adversary agencies outside the Department of Health, Education, and Welfare which will be able to develop balancing viewpoints to the existing system?

TURNER: I believe that there is a tendency in scientific discussions to move off to rather abstract values and assessments,with which I have very little difficulty. But when these are brought back into the real world it troubles me that a federal judge -- who in my profession is considered to be a rather important person -- is able to review the work of a scientist in a regulatory agency and say that it shows a perfect example of garbage in, garbage out in statistics. This was a comment on a decision which allowed vaccines to become available on the market place. The same opinion talks of the horrendous consumer risk that was involved.

The thing that troubles me and the public is not so much the philosophical weighing. I think people would be willing to allow a philosophical weighing of benefits and risks and make their choices if they had the confidence that the facts upon which they were making those decisions and the input into the facts -- the broad data and who decides how to study what -- were done in an open, clear, and accessible way. If that were the case, I believe we would have fewer constraints. And I could even envision a modification of the Delaney clause to some degree if everyone had confidence that those with the responsibility were, in fact, executing it properly.

Unfortunately every single detailed look at the way the responsibilities are executed -- and I say every single one -- indicates that there has been a breakdown of some kind wherever there has been a controversy. Where there is no controversy, where everybody agrees that it is, in fact, a safe and benign problem, or where it is, in fact, a serious problem that we ought to avoid, there is no difficulty -- that is, where we agree as a producer or consumer there is no difficulty. But when we have a producer coming into an official body and saying that if a warning is required that adults should not take a certain chemical the company will have to reconsider whether or not it can be produced because they may not be able to sell it -- when that becomes part of the consideration, then we have moved far outside the scientific realm, and we are in a whole new area where there is great skepticism. I would just submit to you, as you just heard Dr. Wescoe say, that the industry and the FDA have worked out a mechanism whereby they are continuously reevaluated --

WESCOE: Wait a minute. I think that is unfair. I do not think there is any point in saying that. There is no reason why the Food and Drug Administration in its regulatory authority should not be involved with decisions --

TURNER: I did not say there was.

WESCOE: -- as to go or no go at certain times.

TURNER: I did not say that, but what I will say --

WESCOE: You were implying that something was done surreptitiously, that something was done dishonestly by the two sides talking to each other. I have to object.

TURNER: I was not, and I would like to finish what I was saying.

WESCOE: Very good.

TURNER: What concerns me about this, and the point I was trying make, is that there is not a similar mechanism for interests such as the consumer interests to be brought into that kind of a discussion. There have been hundreds and hundreds of meetings between industry and government with which I am perfectly happy, and I agree with your supposition that they should exist. What I am saying is that they should include more parties than merely the producer and the regulator. And that, it seems to me, is the direct answer I would give to Dr. Epstein's questions. Every single time you sit down with the regulatory agency to discuss your product there ought to be an interest from outside the agency and outside the industry participating in that discussion.

(Applause)

WESCOE: As a matter of fact, I believe from the standpoint of what is going on now with the review of the over-the-counter medicines, this is exactly --

TURNER: Yes, and it took us a very long time and a great deal of effort and push to get a consumer and an industry representative on those panels. I think that is an important step forward, and it is the model that I would use as an example. But there is a great deal more needed than merely that. There is no such mechanism in the prescription area. There is not even a mechanism like that in the food additive area. We have been in six months of conversation with the FDA review group on the GRAS list program, and we still have not been able to get a recognition of the fact that there is even an issue about why consumer interests should be involved in that discussion.

I want to clarify one thing. I was not imputing to you, Dr. Wescoe, any kind of bad intention or lack of integrity. What I am saying is that a mechanism that includes two parts of an issue which has many more interests is not a mechanism which will allow us to arrive at a real, clear assessment of what the benefits and risks are.

WESCOE: I was just going to say that when the regulatory agency calls in its advisors from the medical profession -- who, I think, know a great deal more about prescription drugs than do you, Mr. Turner, and I have to say that advisedly -- those people are, in fact, consumers and are presenting at that time a consumer viewpoint. I find that a very fair thing to do. I do not think these things are taken care of in star chamber hearings without there being provided advice from the scientific community, from those who are selected as advisors to the agency.

Just let me say once more that I really do not like the fact that people can be stereotyped. I use as many things as you do, Mr. Turner. I am just as concerned about safety as you are: in fact, I may be even more so. From that standpoint I think we are in complete agreement. I do not think there need be in that circumstance an adversary relationship.

KOSHLAND: Isn't the problem in part caused by the fact that only recently have consumer groups become more organized? Drug companies are organized. Consumer groups are not. Maybe our regulatory agency representative will discuss this later. But are there not more identifiable people in an organized group?

TURNER: That is part of it. I really do not want to have an acrimonious situation. The point is that when we talk about the substance of an issue of science I have no problem with that being a scientific determination. However, when we talk about the procedures whereby that determination is made, I do not believe that is a scientific determination. A star chamber is a legal concept. It is the responsibility of the legal profession and lawyers to define what constitutes a star chamber and what does not. It seems to me that we have a set of procedures that have been designed in the society and generally agreed to by the society for bringing together divergent points of view -- points of view which do exist no matter how much we want to protest that they do not -- to work out whatever the best way of accommodating the various aspects can be. That, it seems to me, is not a scientific question or a physician's question. It is a question of procedures within the entire system, how our society is organized. It is not one from which scientists should be excluded. But on the other hand, it is not one which should be left solely to scientists.

JOSEPH COOPER: Mr. Turner, if you are talking about a pluralistic mechanism for decision making where you can get good balanced inputs, I am all for you. But when you say that we should take the ultimate decision making away from a regulatory agency and put it in the hands of the public, then I do not know.

TURNER: When did I say that?

COOPER: Didn't you say that in the beginning?

TURNER: I do not think I did.

COOPER: You said that it is a public decision, did you not?

TURNER: I look at the regulatory agency as being the agent of the public, not the agent of the producer and not the agent of the consumer, in terms of its identified role. My criticism of it is that it has moved far closer to being the agent of the producer, not because of any venality, particularly, but because of the pressures of the system. It has moved into an ability to deal with their interests better than the interests of the consumers.

COOPER: At one time you might have said that. I think that maybe pre-1962 you could find those influences. However, in recent years I do not think you could find them to any great degree. But that is not really the thrust of what I want to say.

I am not quite clear, but you did say in the beginning that you need a public decision. Did you say that?

TURNER: Yes. I would say that any decision made by the FDA is a public decision.

COOPER: Then do you want some other outside --

TURNER: I was juxtaposing public as opposed to a decision made solely by scientists, and it was a quote from Dr. Weinberg.

COOPER: I see the over-the-counter drug review as a very fine mechanism through which a regulatory agency takes in a diversity of inputs. The one thing on which I have a little hangup, though, is what is a consumer representative. I regard you as a consumer advocate, and I think all who know you would give you high marks on that. I do not necessarily regard you as a consumer representative. Now a lot of us are self-appointed in the roles we take, but what then becomes our technical qualification to make judgments in behalf of the public? There are some very fine distinctions.

TURNER: It depends on what the responsibility of the judgment is. Again, neither of the representatives on the over-the-counter drug panels, for the industry or for the consumer, are there to make scientific determinations. They are there for procedural determinations, and they are designated as liaison members for the purpose of going back to diverse groups within the area they represent, industry or consumer groups, to bring together whatever points of view they think should be put into the mix. In addition to that, both groups are able to nominate people as representatives, as professionals on those panels. Those professional people must meet all of the qualifications for expertise that anybody who is chosen by the FDA must meet. Therefore, we nominate a person whom we would like to see on a panel and who has all those credentials. That person then becomes a member of the scientific body.

The other aspect that we are there for is to ensure that the procedures work to the benefit of the system so that the decision that comes out has had the consideration of all different points of view.

COOPER: I cannot really quarrel with that. I will just wind up on this point. The way it is now is in the public forum, where consumer advocates determine ultimate policy and determine what happens, for example, on cyclamates, either in anticipation or otherwise. That was a political decision. There was never really a chance for scientific judgment to enter into it, even including the National Academy of Sciences inputs. That decision was hurried up. It was one of the most sloppy affairs, and it was all because of a fear of professional consumer advocacy and the reaction to it in the public press. Otherwise, we do not find the kinds of mechanisms to which you so commendably referred. Now, how do we get them?

KOSHLAND: This is a very important point in the design of policy. But I would like to focus more on the future than the past. You are suggesting we need to have some mechanism for greater consumer input before the FDA decision. Is that right?

TURNER: That is right.

KOSHLAND: The practicality of that is the issue on which we should focus.

EPSTEIN: I want to focus the discussion on a wide spectrum of options which should be examined for developing meaningful scientific as well as legal representation of massive national public interest and the consumer interests in the decision making process. It is my basic thesis that the present system at this time largely precludes representation, and that decisions made with the benefit-risk calculus are made in the absence of the balancing viewpoint of the massive national interests affected.

KOSHLAND: We are trying to figure out how we can get a better mechanism.

CLINTON MILLER: I represent the National Health Federation, and my question is addressed to Dr. Wescoe. I also would like Mr. Turner to respond to it. What is your opinion about the consumer who is concerned about the government's requiring that drugs and some substances be too safe? It seems that all the discussion so far has implied that the consumer considers that the regulatory action has not been safe enough. There is a phenomenon going on right now in which it seems that millions of consumers are deeply concerned that the Food and Drug Administration has tried to make vitamins and minerals too safe by reclassifying them as drugs and regulating them as drugs.

I would like your response on this.

WESCOE: I really am not as conversant with the vitamin and the mineral circumstances as I might be, sir. In my opinion, vitamins, inasmuch as they are taken as medicines, are of course drugs, and someone has to be responsible for their regulation.

We had comments by Dr. Handler earlier to the point that even though these things may occur in nature, they are not without their inherent hazards. There has to be some agency concerned with identifying clearly what those hazards are on the basis of the evidence and then making suggestions as to what levels are reasonable so that risks inherent to those products may be kept as low as possible.

I really do not see anything wrong with the Food and Drug Administration being involved in this, because I can conceive of no other agency in the federal government that would be able to look at it from the consumer standpoint other than the Food and Drug Administration.

MILLER: But 99 percent of the consumers who have written to the Food and Drug Administration have said: "You are not protecting us. You are making your requirements too safe when you ban Vitamin C, 100 milligrams, and require it to be classified as a drug."

The Food and Drug Administration has been inclined to represent themselves as a consumer representative when 99 percent of all comments have said to the Food and Drug Administration: You are trying to make it too safe. This is the phenomenon we have to address.

WESCOE: I think there are others who believe from time to time that differences of opinion might be resolved in different and better ways. But I think in this circumstance, since we have an FDA representative still to appear as a speaker, I might let the agency speak for itself.

TURNER: He wants me to give a response. I think that what your question illustrates is that the consumer position is not solely one of saying things should be banned. We are interested, really, in balancing. We are not interested in merely restricting. There has been a suggestion that the unwillingness to take risks inhibits progress. I think we are willing to take risks, but I think only within a framework which is defined and has the right kind of input.

I have spent a long time with the FDA in trying to sort out what they are doing on vitamins. I think as we move through this we will begin to sort out and come to a determination which will distinguish them from the way drugs are regulated at this point.

H. THOMAS AUSTERN: Mr. Turner, coming back to the Delaney clause and cost-benefit within your regulatory public policy ball park, which has seemed to put the

scientists out in left field and also animadverted the regulators. I would like
you to suggest to us who makes the decision as to what Congress meant in enacting
the Delaney clause or what Congress meant when it used those words "if it is found"
or, for that matter, "found to induce," to give you a little more of it. Or does
that word found have any scientific connotation? Might it mean as well that dose
relationship is to be considered? Who finally decides those questions?

TURNER: I think on that last question of whether found implies a dose-relationship
question; I would say that it does not. It does imply, however, that determination, it seems to me, would be a court determination. I do not think there would
be any problem about that.

There are other things about the word found, for example the metabolic activity of the chemical. It may well be that a determination is made that you feed
a chemical to animals and at the other end there is cancer. But it may mean that
there are 20 or 30 intervening causes, and the chemical is not, in fact, the
cause, and so it is not found to be the cause. That, it seems to me, is a scientific determination, one that scientists would make and come to the FDA to report
that this chemical did not cause cancer. On the other hand, you may get a tumor,
and the scientists would look at it and say that it is not a cancerous tumor.
That would be a scientific determination. And it seems to me that is where there
is a great deal of scientific discretion. I do not think on the zero tolerance
question, however, there is any leeway.

AUSTERN: That is as you read the language, but who finally decides?

TURNER: I would say that any interpretation of language is to be made by the court
if there is a controversy. But I do not think that scientists are put out in left

field because of this. That is why I wanted to emphasize scientific determination. It seems to me that where scientists are clear that something did not cause cancer, this is a scientific question which they address. No one is going to come in and say, "You guys do not have the right to do that because we are going to decide in court -- or as a regulatory body or whatever else -- that it did cause cancer."

WESCOE: May I just respond to that by saying that I have in my hands the Congress-ional Record for 1958, and I do not see anything in it that says what Congress meant. There is, as a matter of fact, a complete blank in discussion on that part of the Act that was being considered. There were two men in Congress who stood up to oppose it.

TURNER: Yes. But unfortunately, in 1960 the issue was subjected to congressional hearings and a great deal of review and was reenacted in exactly the same language in another section of the law. It is all spelled out there very clearly.

WESCOE: I am two years ahead of time. Excuse me.

TURNER: I have the quote of Secretary Fleming on that.

WESCOE: I have Secretary Fleming's quote, too.

TURNER: Then he addressed that issue.

WESCOE: But he does not say what it meant.

HOWARD B. HIATT: I would like to ask both Dr. Wescoe and Mr. Turner whether there are policy making mechanisms in these areas in other countries that you think are superior to ours or from which we can learn?

WESCOE: There are policy making mechanisms in other countries relative to medicines. do not really know about mechanisms relating to food additives and other substances.

believe the system in the United States is probably the one that is being used at the present time as a model for others who are moving more seriously into the area of regulation of medicines. I think there is a great deal to be said for the system that is current in the United Kingdom, where there is, I think, just as great an attention to detail but where things are carried on with a great deal more dispatch. This probably relates to the size of the nation, in part, and to the fact that the agency itself has not yet achieved large numbers of personnel to deal with these circumstances.

TURNER: I think essentially the systems are all struggling with the same kinds of procedural questions in terms of how to proceed. I see nothing that is advantageous as a procedural question in any of the ones that I am familiar with. I do like the attitude of the Canadians somewhat better on some issues. DES, for example, for which they found no trace residues, was banned for different reasons. We are bound to residues in our law on DES. The Canadians apparently feel that any chemical that had the kind of effects that DES did in experiments was one that they did not want to have in the meat supply even without residues.

KOSHLAND: Mr. Turner, presumably you cite the Salk vaccine case to suggest that greater care would have avoided some deaths or paralysis. On the other hand, a delay in implementing the vaccine program would have meant a certain larger number of people would have gotten polio.

TURNER: Let me make that analogy very clear before you go on. The warning was discovered six months prior to the incident. When the incident was discovered it took thirty days to correct it and eliminate it. What I am arguing is that there was a six-month leeway where you could have done exactly the same thing on the basis of the three monkeys that you did on --

KOSHLAND: I would rather not get into that case.

TURNER: That is why I used it.

KOSHLAND: The point is whether countries which have more lenient procedures, such as England, have yielded greater benefit earlier than we did, or have they put drugs on the market earlier which caused many more deleterious effects? What is the balance of a country that is more lenient than we are as compared to us?

TURNER: That is a heated debate right now. There is a debate as to whether there is any evidence. There are those who claim that some drugs are used in England which are not used here because of the lack of stringency in England. THe fact that they are being used is being held up as evidence that they are in fact good.

There are others who will argue -- and among them, I think, the FDA is one -- that this is not in fact the case in terms of any health delivery, that in fact the system the United States uses is providing more protection. There have been many instances of hazard abroad that have not been duplicated here, and it is very much a trade-off. Thalidomide is the most dramatic, but there are eight or ten other instances where drugs have gotten through foreign mechanisms and caused problems but did not get through here.

WESCOE: Do you know those instances?

TURNER: Yes. I can get them for you.

WESCOE: I would like them in the record for the sake of accuracy. I do not like unsupported statements.

TURNER: I will put them in.

(See exchange between Turner and Wescoe in chapter entitled Commentary)

WESCOE: A great deal of comment has been made about this issue which has always hinged upon the small phrase "life-saving" drugs. I do not think anyone realistically can say that a "life-saving" drug has been kept from the United States. On the other hand, there may be medicines that provide certain advantages over those available in the United States, some that have certain nuances of action that are not available here. I think they have been adequately tested for safety. May I ask the question that I did not quite understand? Am I entitled to one question? I would like to ask Mr. Turner one because he made a statement that I think might clarify an issue. He said that the National Foundation pushed forward the Salk vaccine. Was that entire decision made by a scientific committee or was it not? It was my impression that the National Foundation had at that time as considerable an input from consumers as it was possible to have?

TURNER: The quote was from Dr. Shannon. He identified the decision as being a scientific one, and he used it in a series of steps from the finding of the isolation of the polio agent until the Sabin vaccine. He argued in his presentation that the scientific advisory committee was meeting without the proper inputs of alternatives and considerations.

DAVID P. RALL: I would like to make a positive suggestion which I hope is not out of place here.

(Laughter)

There was discussion by Dr. Epstein and Mr. Turner about ways of involving representatives of the public and of the consumer in the regulatory decision making process for both food additives and drugs. From what I have seen this would pose very great difficulties. It seems to me there is one way that this could be helped, and that is to make available in a published form all of the information, the data, upon which the regulatory decision is based as soon as that regulatory decision comes out. This would then allow everybody to look at the evidence and see whether the decision was, in fact, a proper one.

TURNER: I endorse that. I think that is absolutely an essential step, and it must be done not only with regulatory agencies but whenever a body is being called as an advisory body or whatever. Their basis of information must be made available. I do not think that the fact that this is a good thing to do, however, necessarily precludes the fact that you could work out systems where there were different points of view, including a consumer point of view, brought into a mechanism.

EPSTEIN: I would like to endorse Dr. Rall's comments. But I would like to point out that essentially what he is suggesting is that one should involve the public and the scientific and legal representatives of the public interest movements and the general scientific community on a post hoc basis. In other words, go ahead, make the decisions, and on a post hoc basis throw the matter open to the whole public debate.

However, this helps create the basis for polarization. Once you enable products to be built into commerce, and once you allow industry to generate irreversible or poorly reversible commitments to these products, and then establish mechanisms for challenging these decisions, you create massive social perturbations.

My view is that it is essential to bring in alternative viewpoints into the decision making process at the earliest possible stage, even before the stage when data are submitted by industry to regulatory agencies. I think one has to go much farther back than this. One has to examine who provides the data, what constraints they are under. How responsive are those who provide the data -- either industry scientists or scientists in commercial testing houses -- how responsive are they to short-term marketing interests? You have to go right back to the beginning. You have to examine how the data were generated and how they are passed on to the agencies. And at all of these stages it is important, if not imperative, that the public interests be appropriately represented.

HARRISON WELLFORD: Dr. Wescoe, you have stated, and I agree, that one can assume that there are safe levels for the kind of cancer causing substances in animals that we are talking about. The problem is that theoretically this is true, but practically in a regulatory context you have the problem of deciding how to determine those thresholds.

You said that animals and men were not the same. A safe threshold in an animal is not necessarily a safe threshold for man. Putting yourself in the position of an FDA regulator who has to make these decisions, how do you suggest that they determine in the regulatory context a safe threshold for these kinds of substances?

WESCOE: I think once more I should let a representative of the Food and Drug Administration speak to that point. Let me say, however, that when we talk about carcinogenicity and mutagenicity we must not overlook the principles of pharmacology and toxicology that have been worked out over a long period of time. The experiments must not become caricatures but must bear some relationship to the reality of human practice if we are to come closer to an answer to this particular question.

There are, I believe, "no effect" levels of these substances. You may not agree with me. There may be many others who do not agree with me also, but I believe experiments do show this. I think there ought to be some control over the laboratories in which they are done.

Dr. Epstein has talked about the constraint of experimental results. In fact, the identity of some of the laboratories in which some of this work has been done has never been revealed. The levels that have been fed have been inordinate. There are, as I said, substances that we use all the time that if fed at enormous levels would show deleterious effects. But I will say this, as a pharmacologist and as a physician also, that such dosages of many substances would kill the animal long before cancer ever appeared.

TURNER: On the issue of convoluted and inappropriate experiments, the Delaney clause itself would allow the exclusion of any evidence that was developed that way. If you came in with an experiment which scientists agreed was not a relevant experiment, it would have no bearing on the Act. The Act expressly excludes it.

WESCOE: I do not read the Act that way.

TURNER: The FDA does.

WESCOE: Really? I do not believe it does. I would like to hear about that later, because I think the clause is specific. There is a part of it that I do not understand, the part which says "in experiments that would seem to be appropriate to the testing of the --"

TURNER: That is the second part of the clause.

WESCOE: I do not know what it means, and I have not heard anybody here yet say what it means either.

TURNER: You see, there is a difference. Let me make one point. There is a difference between saying that the law provides something and saying that you do not understand what the provision is. In other words, if the law says that appropriate tests are required, that is what the law says. Now, if you do not know what an appropriate test is, that is a different question. But you cannot blame the law for that.

(Laughter)

WESCOE: Forgive me. That is the point I usually get back from lawyers.

(Laughter)

TURNER: Seriously, it seems to me that the determination of an appropriate test is quite clearly a scientific determination, and the law has made the provision in the second section of the clause of appropriate test.

WESCOE: No, it does not. Now that, I think, is where I would differ from you, and I do not profess to be an expert in law. The second part of the clause does not say that the first part is not valid. There are two specific parts to it. The first one says --

TURNER: Let us forget it. It is an esoteric and irrelevant discussion.

WESCOE: No, it is neither esoteric nor irrelevant.

KOSHLAND: There is a representative of the FDA here. We have been prodding him to say something, but I think we have finally gotten him out of his seat.

PETER B. HUTT: I am in the delightful position of being able to agree with both of these people.

(Laughter)

There are two parts to the clause. The first part states that if an additive is found to induce cancer when ingested by animals or man, then that substance is illegal. Obviously, therefore, Dr. Wescoe is right. But Mr. Turner also is right in that if the test which showed cancer was a faulty one, then no scientist would find that it had, in fact, induced cancer. So, they are both right.

The second part of the clause states that if cancer is induced upon any other appropriate type of scientific testing which we can determine is a relevant test, a pertinent test, then the substance also is illegal. That again is a scientific issue.

Thus, Congress decided that oral ingestion is inherently relevant and therefore invokes a per se rule, but that in any other type of testing we could exercise scientific discretion to determine whether it is a pertinent test before concluding that the substance is illegal.

OLIVER H. LOWRY: Could I try to answer the question about testing whether or not a drug might produce cancer in man? First, let me stress the fact that living systems do not recognize man-made laws. Regardless of what our written laws say, the cells of the body are going to go ahead and do what they must, according to their own unbreakable laws. It is our job to learn these laws of the cell and proceed accordingly.

Science, fortunately, does not stand still. As we sit here and discuss the problem, and as the present drug laws sit on the books, science is finding ways to answer some of our questions about drug testing. Increasingly it is possible to grow different kinds of human cells in the test tube, and therefore to test drugs on human cells outside of the body. It has long been known that one can produce mutations with certain drugs in these cultured cells. It was once thought that mutation producing activity signified cancer producing activity. This is now known to be not necessarily true. Techniques are becoming available whereby cells exposed to drugs in the test tube can be introduced into experimental animals and tested to see whether cancer cells have been produced. With this and similar techniques it should be possible in the future to provide the kind of quantitative assessment of the cancer hazard of a drug that we cannot give today.

HANS LANDSBERG: Much of what has been said here, I think, focuses on the question of providing information, providing the most information to the consumer in particular so that he can make up his mind. It would save us all a great deal of time and effort if that could be achieved. When we talk about the design of a policy I think it would be very important to try to think about what kind of information the consumer might need to make what we call an intelligent decision about himself. I make a distinction here. He might thereby make a policy decision that concerns not only himself, but let me stick to the individual for a moment.

What kind of information could we give him? What would he need to make such a decision in order that we can shift a great deal of the burden, really, to him from a group like this or a much larger group like this? Now there are two points that have caught my attention.

Mr. Turner, if I understand him correctly, at one point seemed to say that with food additives it just is not feasible because information is so dispersed and so difficult to put together that the consumer would be quite helpless. He might read on a bottle what is in it, but he could not reasonably integrate, add, and keep track of the data. He may not care at all. As far as I am concerned, if he does not care at all, that is his decision.

There was another point which is more interesting. I do not know whether the facts are correct, but as I understand it, a drug producer might say that if he puts certain information on a container the sales may be affected. Therefore, if he cannot sell it, he questions that he should produce it.

Is it not possible that policy might be designed to get around that one, at least, by having an alternate producer? Could not the government in that case buy out the producer and make a drug available as a public service?

TURNER: Let me respond to the first characterization and say that I think you got it exactly backwards. I was saying that with the situation as it now stands, it is impossible for any citizen to select out of his diet FD&C Red No. 2. The first step would be to state its presence on the bottle, can, or whatever. But even if that were done, it is so widespread at this point that you still could not avoid it if you wanted to. So then we have to go to whatever the next step is and begin to think about how we trade off the benefit-risk on a wide basis.

There are many other chemicals, however, which are not that widespread, and which you are not able to choose. Even more important is that there are many chemicals which have effects only on a very small part of the population. That is to me the most important problem. If we can get information out saying here it is, so that people who want to avoid it can avoid it, we have taken our first step toward allowing that individual his own personal self-defense.

LANDSBERG: You have got me forward, not backward.

TURNER: But the point is that I was talking about the situation as it now exists rather than as you implied that I was saying that it was impossible to ever solve this problem. I am saying that the problem as it now exists is amenable to solution.

The second issue, however, is a much more complicated one. The government has on occasion tried to produce vaccines and has not found it to be a task which it could maintain for various reasons. In addition, it is not clear that that would be acceptable in the system that we run which is a profit making system. We have some real problems philosophically.

WESCOE: I think that the entire circumstance that is being discussed now is purely hypothetical. I do not think anybody ever said that issue ever arose, and I suspect that it probably does not.

TURNER: I said that it was, in fact, the case. I quoted from the record of the trial in Philadelphia, and I quoted the manufacturer.

WESCOE: That if the warning were included he would not sell it?

TURNER: No. He did not say he would not sell it. He said that he would have to reconsider making it available to determine whether if the warning was on it he could sell it.

WESCOE: This was the vaccine?

TURNER: Yes. Let me make one other observation in the vaccine area on the mass-inoculation programs. It is a very pecular situation to me, and I think it is something that should be looked into, that the program providing the vaccine also provides the public relations to sell the vaccine. It is sold as a package, and I think that is something that should be thought through very, very carefully in terms of policy. It may well be that one entity should produce the raw material, and then perhaps the government do all the work in selling it.

KOSHLAND: I see lots of hands, and I am very upset about cutting off the discussion, but we must proceed.

I guess the best statement I have seen of risk-benefit analysis was made by Winston Churchill who said, "Behold the turtle. He only makes progress when his neck is out." I think it is quite clear that Joshua Lederberg has made progress and exposed himself to risks both in the field of science and in the field of public policy. It is a great pleasure to welcome him to the Forum.

A System-Analytic Viewpoint*

Joshua Lederberg

Indeed, it is true that anyone who tries to deal with health in economic

terms, which is a necessary part of a system-analytic point of view, is exposing

himself to the risk of misunderstanding and even of bodily harm from outraged

citizens. In a free enterprise society we can defend the incentives needed to

reinforce the work-ethic in terms like depriving the poor of caviar and champagne;

but we balk at cold-bloodedly depriving them of an artificial kidney or of a life-

saving drug when these therapeutic benefits have become validated and available to

the wealthy. Public attitudes about accelerating the availability of new drugs

for anyone's benefit are more ambivalent, involving a conflict of values. This is

precisely why we came together for this Forum.

The arousal of conscience about health is one of the major impulses toward

more egalitarian redistribution of income, an ideological issue often confused with

the technical ones of drug safety and of efficacious organization of health serv-

ices.[1] The question of the proper dollar equivalent of a human life also often

---

* This text is an edited version of the transcript of the address as presented
at the Forum. I spoke from rough notes at that time, and other exigencies
detained me from preparing a more definitive statement without unduly delaying
this publication. A more carefully argued and documented version will be published elsewhere and may well show signs of further evolution in my views.
                                                                    --Author

(1) At least the canons of welfare economics separate the allocation of investments for a potential pareto optimum from the redistribution needed to achieve
goals of social justice. The latter is the task for tax legislation or welfare assistance. However, political optima are not automatically achieved;
in the real world some sacrifice of ideal productivity may be essential to
achieve the political harmony which is in turn indispensable for economic
efficiency.

comes up in these discussions; to my view, most such calculations are absolute nonsense.

The net crude social value of an individual's life is measured economically by the effect of his death on the net products left to the community. Calculations based on his still unrealized earnings are faulted by their neglect of the individual's consumption. To the extent that the worker has struck a fair bargain with his employers and with the Internal Revenue Service, he will on the average be consuming approximately what he is worth. We would have to conclude that the average net social value of a life is approximately zero!

Individual cases will show wide excursions, even short of the incalculable values attached to the lives of saints or dictators. Estate taxes will have been discounted in workers' bargains; but their premature collection is a social benefit. By this logic of the absurd, so is the demise of a superannuated beneficiary of Medicare. On the other hand, the death of the exploited worker who may consume less than his individual product would be a social loss, except when he is readily replaced in a less than full employment economy. We do not, in fact, deal with our fellowmen simply as units of production; these calculations take no account of the costs incurred by "nonproductive" survivors such as spouses and children. Since we have incurred a social obligation for their welfare, the transfer of their support to the community generates a social loss upon the death of a provider. (These losses already will have been socialized through the taxes incurred on wages during viable employment.)

From another angle we can see that each generation is subsidized by the undepreciated capital savings of its predecessor--its farms, houses, factories, fortresses, and libraries--and taxed by the depletion of unrenewable resources. If an economic measure is possible in these terms, the tangible values of human life might be calculated closer to the loss of anticipated future savings rather than of earnings.

All of these calculations of crude social value of life aggregate the interest of the community, but they ignore the welfare of the most interested person, namely the decedent. We are a society composed entirely of prospective decedents. Indeed, the collective aversion of risks of death and disease is a central function of social organization. From this standpoint there can hardly be a "proper" absolute value of life; we go through economic calculations only in order to achieve the most efficient _relative_ allocation of resources in protecting our most precious goods. It may be misleading to use dollars as the currency for these evaluations. But unless we have some common measure for assessing risks, we will be spending disproportionate parts of our concern and energy for isolated parts of the overall problem of life, while neglecting others possibly more important. Our analysis is then entirely dedicated to helping us optimize the bargains that we need to make in gambling against fate.

In another context I have tried to estimate the dollar hazards of radiation side-effects in connection with the controversy about nuclear power. This calculation needed two estimates. The kind of dollars-for-health bargain that we strike in other contexts is a _social_ judgment that can be observed rather than edicted. The health consequence of a given dose of radiation is a _technical_ judgment about which there is a more convergent consensus than one would guess from a debate that has mixed it with social prescriptions. For the former I postulated that we might be willing to double our health expenditures for 20 percent improvement in health. This would imply a social willingness to invest $400,000 to prevent a death, which is at the high side of present day political judgments. The latter is too complex to detail here.[2] I found that a number like $100 per person per rem exposure

---

(2) See J. Lederberg, "Squaring an Infinite Circle: Radiobiology and the Value of Life," _Bulletin of the Atomic Scientists_ 27 (September, 1971): 43-45; and L. A. Sagan, "The Human Costs of Nuclear Power," _Science_ 177 (August 11, 1972): 487-493.

came close to the intersection of many different actual policies which we use in coping with radiation exposure. For example, this says that the natural background of radiation already inflects a per capita health cost of about $10 per year, and that we also pay about $5 in health side-effects (about the same in dollars to the radiologist) for our medical diagnostic X-rays. Generally, we expect X-ray diagnosis to be an advantageous bargain, although not of course when there is avoidable exposure to radiation without corresponding medical benefit.

People could quarrel with these numbers, but they might then be impelled to apply whatever number they arrived at consistently to a variety of policy decisions. If one could do as well with drugs and food additives, we would be much closer to a rational foundation for regulatory policies. The results of my personal inquiry remain primitive and elusive; and I feel a bit of a fraud in using the term system-analytic in my title, except insofar as a view is mostly in the eyes of the beholder.

We are in deep trouble both on the cost and benefit side at a primary level, and even worse when it comes to judging the impact of possible diseconomies of investment and innovation in the field of drugs and environmental additives.

A pricing of benefits for food additives is theoretically straightforward, and I cannot agree with Dr. Wescoe that we would discard a flavor or a color on acount of any risk no matter how slight. We would have to discard every additive automatically and out of hand. For there simply is no way to assure that the risk of any substance or process is really zero. When one refers to zero risk he usually has some practical level of risk in mind, and it is our task to make such calculations explicit. Only then can we make the trade-offs rational and our policies publicly persuasive.

The pricing of food additive benefits is not just their annual market value, about $1/2 billion a year, although this is one term in the equation. The consumer's net benefit is measured by the difference in the price of his purchases with and without the additives, if he is indifferent to their presence, plus or minus his market judgment[3] of their value when he knows they are there. Many additives are substitutes for natural food substances over which they may have only marginal economical advantage. For these the consumer benefit is much smaller than the size of the market and may approach zero. Others effectively reduce the price of food, for example by retarding spoilage or allowing convenient formulations not otherwise attainable. The production of food entails its own risk of life; hence to eschew economic advantages in the face of "any risk" may be as inhumane as it is ineffi-cient. The reasonable question to ask is whether the benefits of a particular additive are commensurate with its possibly insidious risk to health. We need to bring these estimates out on the table, and of course they must be particularized substance by substance.

If the consumer also had the information to judge these risks, as well as consult his tastes, we might let the marketplace take the role of the Food and Drug Administration. The consumer could then calculate his own dollar equivalent of the implied risks. But we democratically have decided to collectivize such decisions. Against the lost advantages of the pricing mechanism, we must weigh the cost of put-ting this information into every consumer's hands product by product; his vulnera-bility to persuasion by mass advertising; and the disorganization of consumer interests as compared to producers', except via government. (Indeed the most per-plexing issue in my reading of welfare economics is the role of advertising which is dedicated to the production of wants rather than of goods.)

---

(3) But here's the rub. The concept of the "consumer's surplus" is easier to enunciate than is any practical measurement. We have no laboratory where the price-elasticity of demand can be empirically measured without the intervention of a host of confounding factors. But most economic theory is based upon similar operationally inaccessible idealizations.

When we turn to drugs we face even more perplexing problems of assessing their benefits, since life and health are prominent terms on both sides of the equation. To start with, however, we can ask how drug prices are in fact determined and on what relationship to consumer benefits and the usual mechanisms of the marketplace.

Drugs cost so little compared to other health services (about 10 percent of health care expenditures) that I suspect their pricing is more akin to that of the cosmetics and the perfumes which accompany them at the retail counter than the pricing of tangible articles of commerce such as bread and automobiles. Howbeit a small private "tax" on these sales, less than you pay the government on your tobacco and your alcohol, supports the research and development of the drug companies in their competitive efforts to produce new products for the benefit of the consumers, and for their own benefit in beating out their fellows. At these prices a significant part of the cost of a drug may in fact not be its retail dollar price but its unwanted side-effects. We must learn to measure these for equity to the consumer and for assurance that we do not waste the precious resource of exposure to risk without achieving commensurate gains. In fact, we are in a sense trying to find the "optimum" number of casualties that should be associated with the use of new beneficial agents.

We could claim to aspire to zero risk, but this is unachievable in the real world. If that seems harsh, and this is precisely the analogy that has been used before, try to think of the ways that the automobile casualty rate could be reduced to zero. Of course, in principle it could be: for example, if a policeman on every block kept our speed down to a few miles per hour and periodically checked the state of our blood alcohol. But there is no way short of a total ban on new drugs or a system of infringement on personal behavior comparable to the analogy that I mentioned for the automobile through which we can achieve perfect safety or even predict and anticipate every possible side-effect.

Our problem is to find a point of balance in the costs and benefits of drugs not where the advantage of a drug exceeds its price plus its hazards, which may always be true, but where further investment in development no longer leads to a commensurate yield in the aversion of risk and the enhancement of efficacy.

This is the familiar concept of marginal utility applied to drug development, and we should not be bedazzled by the undoubted absolute benefits of many drugs in seeking to find the optimal position of investment that must be made in verifying their efficacy and their safety.

Part of the investment cost is the deferral of benefit from the use of a drug while awaiting the outcome of further testing. This includes patients' benefits as well as producers' profits. For major therapeutic discoveries, such as some anti-biotics, this cost conceivably could outweigh all the others; but I am confident that this is already in the minds of the regulatory agencies as well as of the other parties to these concerns.

A crude model of the drug R&D process is summarized in Figures 1 and 2. For these printed versions, extensive captions take the place of the pointer talk at the oral presentation.

Figure 1 is an idealized version of progressive investment in a drug research program. In reality it would be more appropriate for the engineering design of an electronic component, for it supposes the opportunity of progressive chemical modification leading to an ever better product. This hoped for objective improvement is measured by the net utility, the therapeutic benefit less the drug cost and less side-effects. The estimates of these parameters are subject to consider-able uncertainty, expressed in Figure 2 as probability distributions. Especially since the Kefauver amendments, a very large part of drug research investment is

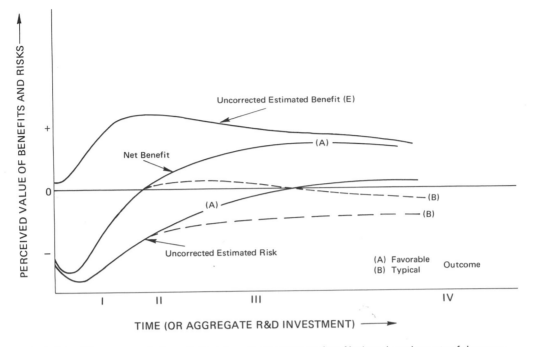

FIGURE 1: *Time course of a hypothetical drug development project.* Neglected are the costs of drug production, variances in the estimates (see Figure 2), and decreases in benefit because of the time value of money and of delayed patient access to the drug.

At point zero (no empirical data yet) there is a negligible presumption of utility and some presumption of risk. At I, evidence of specific biological activity should deepen the suspicion of risk. But a successful drug discovery will move to II, where further chemical refinement as well as knowledge of proper dosage, etc., reduces the risk, and the benefits can be foreseen. However, net benefit can still increase with further investment. This can, of course, also result in more efficient production processes and in turn lower the consumer's cost. R&D should continue to point III, where the slope of the net benefit curve equals the rate of investment. If continued to IV, there is a diminishing return with asymptotic refinement of the risk estimate.

Meanwhile, the gross benefit may fluctuate also. In this case, it may even decline with time owing to the eventual introduction of competing substitutes.

The drug might rationally be accepted at any point after II (but see Figure 2). Further R&D may be necessary mainly to determine whether the drug continues to confer net benefits relative to potential substitutes (compare cases A and B). At issue is the relative social utility of more information about this product compared, e.g., to research investments in a "next generation" of other substances. Unless safety is somehow monetized, the market mechanism may not motivate such investments. The impetus is left either to government or to the professional prescribers—and the latter's time may be too costly for unorganized responses to be effective.

The real payoff of further safety research is the discovery of unsuspected hazards that may lead to disapproval of the drug. This social gain is, of course, in direct conflict with the interest of the promoter who by now has invested much sweat, tears, money, perhaps even blood in the project.

Further delay in the introduction of products might be mitigated if we had other ways to ensure the vigilant scrutiny of a drug by disinterested parties after it has been marketed. The hazard is that by now the promoter may have trebled his investment between R&D and marketing. The shrewdness of drug developers in anticipating the further course of their investigations of safety and of benefit will, of course, have an enormous impact on the average development cost per successful drug that reaches the market. Equally contributory will be the style of the regulatory agency in posing criteria for acceptance that are relevant to the social utility of the drug's introduction.

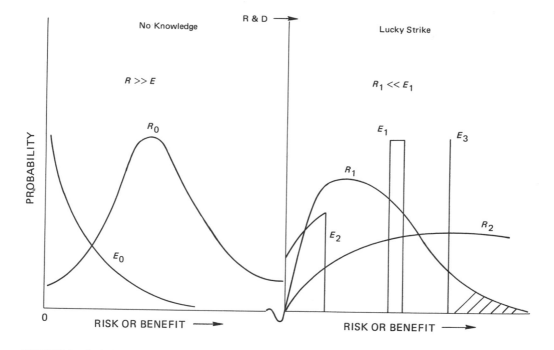

FIGURE 2: *Probability distribution of risk and efficiency in a successful case.* E_1 and R_1 on the right correspond to point II of the previous figure. The efficacy E_1 is assumed to be known with great precision in the context of controlled trials. However, this is an idealization for most drugs when alternative therapies are also considered. Besides the residual uncertainty in the risk distribution R_1, the regulator must also take account of real-world degradation in the criteria and conditions of use of an approved drug, which may correspond to E_2 and R_2. To assure a net social gain, he may demand that the more stringent criterion E_3 be satisfied. The patients of superior doctors are doubtless penalized in this way by the performance of the less qualified because of the lack of effective monitoring on prescribing behavior.

concerned with the validation of a product in which the promoter already has a high stake, rather than the work leading to its primary discovery. Part of our task is to determine the optimum allocation of resources between these creative versus critical efforts. Our social policies must give priority to first order consumer benefits and risks. But we cannot neglect the incentives and rewards needed to motivate producers to risk their fortunes in seeking new drugs from which future consumers may also benefit.

Insofar as drug research tends to become ever more costly as it moves from the chemical laboratory bench to animal testing and to clinical trials, the early anticipation of possible faults can have an enormous influence on the efficiency of the research process. I am not aware of any systematic analyses of the allocation of research resources within the drug industry to these various stages of development. Dr. Gerald Lauback, president of the Pfizer Company, has commented that the batting average of success in new drug applications varies considerably from company to company. I would surmise that this is in part a consequence of the shrewdness of research strategies. However, other factors, such as accidents of change of policy with time or the different criteria applicable to drugs in different fields, may also play a very important role. In any event, one can hardly assess the cost-efficiency of the regulatory procedure without also addressing the pragmatic efficacy of the industry's response to it. In fact, the most passionate complaints that have been voiced from industry sources have been addressed not so much to the principles of drug regulation itself, which have become accepted parts of social policy to a very large degree, but rather to the bureaucratic framework in which these policies are actually implemented. But this also is a subject about which it is obviously difficult to obtain credible information for public scrutiny or to arouse public attention.

Once a drug has been developed to the point where it appears to be a promising candidate for more detailed benefit and risk evaluation, it is submitted to the critical process which is symbolized by Figure 2. Many other candidates, of course, fall by the wayside, but there are few public statistics to help us fit numbers to the parameters of our system design. Our prior state of knowledge about a compound likely to be found in the inventory of a drug company is that, having some biological activity, it is quite likely to be <u>harmful</u>; we can hardly posit that it would be <u>useful</u> without further studies. When it has reached the point of nominal acceptability, the probable benefit exceeding the probable risk, the distributions describing these parameters may resemble E_1 and R_1 respectively of Figure 2. Within the framework of a controlled trial the benefits may be rather well understood; and I have indicated this by showing E_1 as a spike with negligible variance. Risks tend to be more elusive to evaluate, especially the long-term side-effects, such as cancer or mutagenesis, which are such an important preoccupation today. R_1 is therefore indicated with a higher dispersion. Provided one has evaluated E_1 and R_1 not in a vacuum, but in relation to other therapeutic alternatives already available, the acceptance point for a drug rationally should be just when its aggregate benefits exceed the aggregate risks.

In practice this would be highly unpersuasive to an official with regulatory responsibility for a number of reasons, some of which are socially beneficial and some merely characteristic of the bureaucrat's environment. To take up the latter first, it is perfectly obvious that his calculus of risks must include his far greater vulnerability for criticism if the expectations, however reasonable, of risks > benefit should fail; politically they will not be balanced as they are statistically by an equal number of circumstances where the contrary holds. Therefore, to protect his own position he is sure to demand a much more rigorous criterion than would be necessitated by an analytical view of social welfare. His characteristic management tool for this purpose is simply <u>delay</u>.

This bias is strongly reinforced by more rational arguments of public interest. The inertia of drug replacement, particularly within a given firm, is such
that the early approval of a barely adequate agent may delay the effort needed to
bring about far superior introductions. Experience has shown a secular trend
favoring early optimism and later disillusion for many drugs. Once the drug has
been approved, the information gathering environment will be altered, sometimes
irreversibly. Finally, it is necessary to extrapolate from the statistics derived
from controlled clinical trials to those which will pertain when the drug is
generally available. With rare exceptions this must result in a considerable deter-
ioration of the benefit-cost ratio, if for no other reason that in the real world
therapeutic environment the drug will be used in more complicated cases and sometimes by less critical prescribers. These shifts are indicated by the curves E_2
and R_2; the regulator is certain to require a shift in the criterion relative to
risk represented by E_3. At the present time we have no common understanding, much
less agreement, about the appropriate size of that shift even in principle. This
is, of course, further confounded by the practical difficulties of arriving at numbers to match these general concepts. The fact remains that drug developers are
working in a policy vacuum with respect to the criteria that their products are
expected to meet. The concept "safe," so blithely mentioned in law and in popular
discussion, remains an essentially subjective judgment relative to possible
benefits.

Figure 3 addresses a more technical problem with respect to the assessment of
risk. Routine toxicological screening is likely to eliminate those agents showing
a high order of toxicity. If by chance man should prove to be an unusually susceptible species, this also will be discovered during clinical trials or soon after
the introduction of a new agent. Existing procedures appear to be well adapted
to identifying such high level risks, and in the absence of unusually bad luck will

78

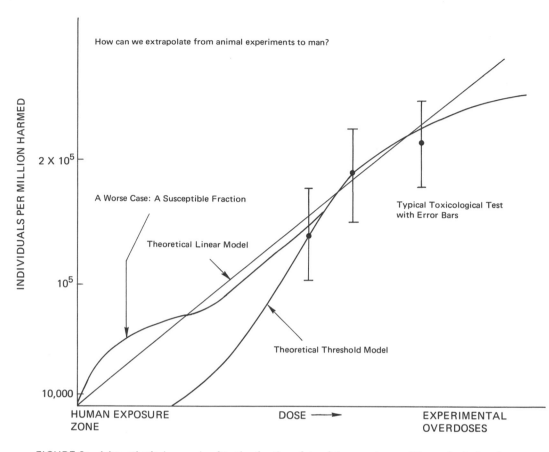

FIGURE 3: *A hypothetical example of testing for the safety of drugs under conditions of calculated over-dosages.* It is difficult to do animal experiments where fewer than 10 percent of the animals respond. In order to satisfy this criterion, it inevitably may be necessary to use levels of a drug (or food additive) far in excess of that which would pertain to human usage. The most reasonable estimate of the level of human response is then highly dependent on the model adopted for drug effect as a functional dose. The arrow-bars shown on the two experimental points are not unreasonable for practical experimentation and might indeed be relatively even larger at lower levels of effect. Therefore, the failure to discover a toxic effect on a limited number of animals at a lower dose is unable to prove the safety of the agent for widespread human consumption, and we must rely on some theoretical rationale, or on experimental evidence, for the dose-effect model. For most purposes, the linear model may be appropriate in the absence of other knowledge. In some circumstances a threshold model can be justified which would be reassuring with respect to human susceptibility at lower doses. On the other hand, the occurrence of a minority of individuals with unusual susceptibility is an alarming alternative. This susceptibility may be the result of genetic variation, interaction with other drugs and environmental agents, or the disease states themselves. While data from drug overdosage may lead to distorted estimates of the safety of an agent, errors in either direction are equally likely, and results from such tests should be regarded as a starting point of further investigation, especially if deleterious results are achieved. In some cases, however, it may be quite possible to authenticate the validity of a threshold model by experimental evidence, and this certainly should be accepted in any reasonable system of assessment of probable drug hazards. On the other hand, much ingenuity is required to suggest a range of animals, of their genetic variation, and of environmental contexts for the testing of drugs that can begin to simulate the conditions of exposure of the human population. For these reasons it is probably untrue that animal testing can predict all possible human hazards. It therefore must be supplemented by more careful epidemiological scrutiny than is possible at the present time. In many cases metabolic analysis should be as reliable a predictor of potential trouble spots as the purely empirical testing for toxicity which is now mandated.

be able to anticipate them before there has been appreciable human exposure.

More insidious problems arise from compounds which have a low order of toxicity or which may take many months or years before they exert toxic effects in man. The most striking and perhaps most frightening example is the dye stuff intermediate, beta-naphthylamine, which has been responsible for epidemics of bladder cancers among chemical factory workers. Epidemiological studies here showed that a large proportion of workers who were chronically exposed were at risk of bladder cancer that appeared only after an interval of 10 to 15 years following initial exposure. The more recent discovery that the therapeutic synthetic hormone, DES, taken by mothers during pregnancy could induce the appearance of vaginal cancer in their daughters 15 or 20 years later is an object lesson of comparable dimensions. And the thalidomide tragedy, of course, has been the turning point for political attention to the problem of drug safety.

The unhappy truth is that none of the regulatory procedures that have been developed with the intention of responding to these threats is likely to be a particularly effective means of preventing similar mishaps in the future! None of these forms of toxicity had a well-established base of scientific knowledge or of biological detection prior to their occurrence as a human disaster. After the fact it has been possible to develop test systems that might have indicated some reason for caution for any of these agents, but their specificity and efficacy are subject to very serious doubt. The principal measure that would have some hope of minimizing the health impact of hazardous introductions, or for that matter of natural or synthetic compounds already in long use, would be a systematic collection of health data which has been strenuously resisted by civil libertarians on the grounds of possible abuses of privacy. Half-way measures, such as voluntary reporting of adverse drug effects, have been initiated, and if they are vigorously pursued may be some help in addressing the problem. But the principal emphasis in enforcing safety testing has been on work with animals along lines that tend to encourage the large-scale collection of routine data rather than the establishment of creative investigations that look for problems on the basis of some theoretical rationale. Such procedures are likely to err in both directions because of the very serious difficulties of extrapolating from animal to the human context. Many dangerous compounds will be overlooked, or their hazards underestimated; on the other hand, many substances whose benefit-risk ratio is in fact highly advantageous for human use may be unfairly excluded.

One possible remedy would be to introduce another stage in the introduction of a drug intended for widespread use, namely its initial availability to a somewhat limited group of practitioners who have the necessary qualifications of education and experience to assist in the assessment of a new drug applied in practice to large numbers of patients, and who have a moral and legal obligation to cooperate in such an evaluation. Although such a procedure has no specific legislative authorization, something closely akin to it was adopted for the introduction of L-dopa for the treatment of Parkinson's disease with results that have been the source of widespread congratulation as an innovative procedural step, as well as a more sober appreciation of the benefits and the side-effects of the drug. Meanwhile, for many drugs we must make do the best we can with animal experiments, attempting to gain the outmost possible by way of prediction of human hazard.

A thorough analysis of the predictive value of animal data, and the limitations that arise from many sources, has yet to be made. It is perfectly obvious that the literal language of the Delaney amendment, which would forbid the use of a food additive (but not a drug!) upon any evidence that it could cause cancer in any animal when fed to any degree, has no scientific justification. It is certain that there are many natural food constituents that would eventually have to be disqualified also under a literal reading of the language of that law. In recent years, it has become perfectly evident, however, that scientific judgment in the interpretation of the significance of animal findings does play a role in the regulatory procedure; the potential threat of arbitrary exclusions of compounds under the Delaney principle will be better remedied by improvements in the scientific cogency of such judgments than by changes in legal phraseology. And Mr. Hutt, speaking from this same platform, has pointed out that most if not all of the regulatory actions that concerned the cancer potential of food additives have been justified by the general responsibility of FDA for food safety and did not depend on the Delaney amendment per se. Since it has been known for many years that food as such can induce cancer--that is to say that underfed animals tend to have lower rates of cancer in general--it is obvious that a great deal of scientific judgment must enter into the evaluation of the risks to human health that may be pointed to by animal experiments with specific additives.

While routine testing, often demanded in a number of species, may result in very costly expenditures for the validation of an additive or a drug, current regulations do not require thoughtful analysis of the metabolism of a new agent. Indeed, the diversion of funds for rote private testing is a positive deterrent to the rational investigation of a proposed new compound. With metabolic information it will often be possible for insightful investigators to formulate hypotheses of possible sources of trouble that could lead to critical tests likely to be far more cost-effective than the current procedures. For example, cyclamates may well go through several cycles of review on account of their economic importance--less to the producers than to food processors--and also in response, perhaps, to the wants of a segment of the consumer public. To undertake costly experimentation on still more batches of rates with cyclamate itself is not very close to the point in view of recent knowledge that the likely source of the chronic toxicity of of this sweetener is almost certainly the metabolic product cyclohexylamine. Whatever the disposition of this compound in rodents, it is clear that a proportion of human beings eventually metabolize cyclamate to yield cyclohexylamine, perhaps with the help of modified intestinal flora that develop during chronic feeding with this agent. The testing of cyclohexylamine, and its further oxidation products, is likely to lead to a decisive understanding of the level of risk associated with cyclamate far sooner and at much less cost than continued agonies with the original raw material. In view of the demonstration of N-hydroxylcyclohexylamine as a metabolite of cyclamate, and the chemical analogies of this compound with other biologically active and vicious derivatives of hydroxylamine, the outcome of such experiments is to some degree predictable but not yet their actual quantitative impact.

With this as with many other products we face the following dilemma in establishing empirical protocols. Most food additives and many drugs offer benefits that may be very large in the aggregate but would still not be worth the risk of substantial mortality arising from their use. Few people would defend the continued availability of a food additive that could be predicted, for example, to result in say 100 deaths per year. But for a consumer population of, say, 100 million, we must be able to rule out toxic side-effects to a level of 1 per million exposed even to meet that criterion! There is simply no way to measure toxicities at that level with animals. Tests within the more nearly feasible range of 100 to 1,000 animals might well give a result of zero mortality, that is to say less than 1 per 1,000, without revealing a level of population risk that would be absolutely intolerable. Such discussions have been muddled by the assertion of the concept of a "no effect dose" in the absence of experimental and statistical procedures to demonstrate that "no effect" actually falls below the level of our policy concern.

What we are ordinarily obliged to do is revealed in Figure 3. In order to bring the level of perceptible effect within the scope of the statistics of a laboratory experiment, we consciously overdose the test animals at levels of 10, 100, or even thousands of times higher than would be the exposure of the human population. On the simplest assumption there might be a proportional relationship between the observed toxicity and the concentration of the agent used, and we might then hope to establish rates of toxic side-effect that could then be used for policy purposes. This would be indicated in Figure 3 by the straightforward linear extrapolation.

This is not necessarily the way a particular agent works. Indeed, for certain types of toxic effect it is reasonable to suppose that lower doses can be accommodated by the metabolic machinery of the subject in such a way that the harm to each individual is negligible and the serious or lethal outcome most unlikely to occur. Agents that are direct cellular poisons, or that influence processes like transmission of the nerve impulse, may well fall in this category.

On the other hand, there are many compounds whose effect on the cell is believed to be quantal, all or none. This applies particularly to mutagenic agents and probably likewise to carcinogens. Here a single molecule, attaching to a vital target, may be the ultimate agency of harm. Then the dose effect relationship boils down to the statistical probability of a given molecule being able to reach a specific molecular target. Although the body could well tolerate the eradication of a substantial number of single cells, if one of them effectively becomes a cancer clone, this may be sufficient to eventually kill the host. For such agents a linear relationship between lethal probability and dose is entirely reasonable on theoretical grounds. This model also is admittedly oversimplified. The metabolism of the compound before it reaches its eventual target may well be different at lower and at higher doses, as well as between specific experimental animal species and man.

While these effects may tend to exaggerate the toxicity of an agent at low levels, there are other phenomena, such as metabolic variation among individuals and interactions with other chemicals and with disease states, that would operate in a more grievous direction. The extrapolation from high doses to low ones by a linear function therefore would appear to be entirely justified as a first order procedure, but one that ought to be susceptible to criticism and rebuttal if additional experimental information is afforded. The production of tumors in mice with high doses of cyclamates is provocative rather than conclusive evidence that a lower but proportional rate of cancer would be produced at a lower level of this agent. But it is a warning that needs to be respected until and unless explicit contrary information can be exhibited that shows that the toxic side-effect is more than proportionally reduced at lower doses of the agent. And in this case, of course, we would have to pay close attention to existing knowledge of the metabolism of the agent.

Unhappily we have really no very satisfactory examples of empirical studies on the toxicity-dose relationship of food additives or drugs. The accumulation of evidence for carcinogens like the polycyclic hydrocarbons cautions us that the situation is, to say the least, quite complicated; and these studies also do not exclude a variety of intervening variables like cigarette smoking and individual variability. A widely observed effect with carcinogenic substances is not only a reduction in the frequency of the tumor lesions with lower doses, but a prolongation of the latent period before they become established. This finding tends to speak for a systemic as well as a cellular component in the toxicity of these agents, and similar remarks can be made for radiation. The model that is often evoked is that a carcinogen, besides initiating a tumor clone, must also interact with some induced or spontaneous depression of the mechanism of immune surveillance before the cancer can be expressed. We will face great difficulties, of course, in evaluating chemical substances for carcinogenesis as long as we remain so ignorant of the mechanisms by which they operate. However, these very complexities offer little reassurance about the security with which new agents can be used because they point to the possible interaction with a wide variety of other environmental circumstances which inevitably occur in the overall human population and which would be impossible to deal with in controlled experiments.

One example has been published of dose effect relationships with a chemical carcinogen namely beta-naphthylamine, the substance already mentioned as a cause of bladder cancer. In an attempt at quantitative dose effect study, Conzelman and Moulton were able to induce bladder tumors in 24 out of 34 dogs exposed to beta-naphthylamine for periods of 6 to 26 months. At the levels used many of the dogs had multiple tumors, a fact that taken together with the limited number of animals makes it difficult to draw quantitative conclusions about the dose effect relation-ship. They obtained numerous tumors, however, after more extensive latent periods, with the lowest dose levels--6mg/kg body weight daily--and believe they had indica-tions that a given total dose was even more effective if administered over a longer period of time. Such a result is theoretically reasonable in circumstances where the initial compound must be metabolized to yield the final cancer producing product and where the metabolic system for doing this may become saturated. However, the data in this and other cases are still too scanty to justify the drawing of general conclusions at this time.[4]

---

(4) It should be noted that the FDA has adopted a quantitative definition of safety in its recent proposed regulations for analytical termination of residual hormones used in animal feeds. In effect, these regulations require standards that can be justified as resulting in a risk of not greater than one per 100 million consumers exposed in practice. The severity of this standard is somewhat mitigated by being based on the assumption that men and mice will respond to cancer at the same rate at a given concentration of carcinogen in their diets. While some mouse strains have been bred for high sensitivity to cancer, the rapid metabolism of the mouse, its shorter life span, and its smaller target volume may theoretically make it rather less sensitive a unit than is the human. We have no experimental data that would enable this point to be criticized empirically.

The Kefauver amendments of 1962 may be thought of as a social experiment that itself deserves critical evaluation; can the procedures of rigorous prior testing of drugs be verified to be both safe and efficacious, the criteria that the drugs themselves must meet? Dr. Sam Peltzman, professor of economics at UCLA, has attempted such an evaluation which has received some notice through Milton Friedman's column in Newsweek and through testimony before the Nelson Committee. The data he uses are essentially those appearing in Figure 4. They are historical and economic analyses of what has happened to drug introductions in the United States since the time of the Kefauver explosion of concern about safety and efficacy, and we will divide drugs into old, or pre-Kefauver, and new, or post-Kefauver. It is perfectly obvious that there has been a drastic reduction in the number of new chemical entities that have been introduced in the United States since that period. It is reasonable, although by no means proven, that the rigors of testing are an important reason both from the standpoint of rejection of candidates and the cost-deterrence to proceeding with certain lines of innovational effort. Commensurate with that reduction, there has been a very large escalation in the average investment per successful drug outcome. (These data only go up until 1968. I simply have not been able to find any more recent information.)

Now Peltzman does not firsthand make a statement as to whether this is good or bad. He is asking a question as to whether there are methods of assessing the social utility of this increase in development cost per drug on the market from something like $5 million per new agent in 1960, to what must be approaching $50 or more million. Are we getting anything for this? Peltzman says that he does not know anything about medicine, but that as an economist he will ask about market behavior; if a new regime of rigorous testing has resulted in more efficacious products, then these "new" drugs ought to be competing more favorably than old ones in a marketplace which is presumably dominated by expert consumers, namely physicians.

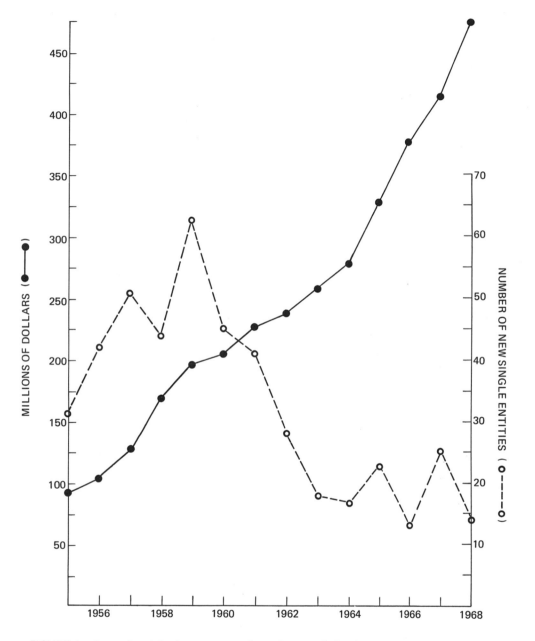

FIGURE 4: *Research and development expenditures for prescription drugs versus basic new products introduced from 1955 to 1968.* Source: National Institute of Neurological Diseases and Stroke, Section on Epilepsy.

His finding is that their behavior is about the same. This is to say with respect to the life cycle of the drug, to its market share, to the other economic measures he has been able to adduce, that the drugs which have successfully passed this tight filter of the post-Kefauver area have fared no better in the judgment of physicians than the ones that were there before.

His model might be summarized as saying that it appears as if there is a constant number of entities on the market at any one time, that they are simply turning over more slowly at the present time than before, and that the more recent introductions are showing no unique behavior in professional market response than the previous ones. I have not examined his assertions in any great detail, but even if they are granted, there are other possible interpretations. They are either very praiseworthy or very pejorative about the physicians who are making the basic consumer choices. You could say, for example, to explain these results that prescribing-behavior is <u>random</u>: that it has no relationship to the therapeutic efficacy of various agents, that the reason the new ones are doing no better than the old on the market is that in spite of having been screened more carefully for therapeutic efficiency, the doctors are choosing them at random or they are being selected for advertising on criteria that have no relationship to therapeutic use.

Alternatively, in the post-Kefauver era, many physicians are approaching a state of rational therapeutic nihilism: that is, one of very great skepticism about drugs in general, but especially skepticism about new introductions even if the FDA has certified them with respect to efficacy and safety. They are relying on the drugs that they have learned to love and learned to trust over long periods of use. This resistance to change now compensates for asserted advantages of the new agents so that they remain more or less at par.

Many other models are, of course, entirely possible to try to interpret what has been going on both with respect to innovation and to these choices. If the rate of therapeutic innovation seems to be slowing down, many other aspects of national life are much less exuberant today than they were in 1960, and must be for very different kinds of reasons. This is not to dismiss the problems of loss of incentive about which many industry people have been agonizing. They believe that it is becoming increasingly difficult to rationalize the sinking of research funds into very long-term projects which may require even 15 or 20 years before a profitable return can be anticipated. Drug companies are obviously not going broke in large numbers; but that is a different question from whether they have the motivation to invest their resources in creative research. It is far safer to concentrate on marketing and on the kinds of research that may have a more immediately visible and early payoff--the so-called "me too" syndrome.

In any case, there is the possibility that by raising the price of admission to the drug production game, the Kefauver amendments must have worked to reduce competition and favor a monopolistic trend. There can be no retreat from the principle of demanding and somehow paying for critical research needed to ensure a high quality of new drugs. The urgent problem is to identify the waste in these procedures, especially to bring the drug development cycle back to a reasonable time.

In an ideal market system these matters would be of less concern. The retail price of new, effective drugs would indeed be encumbered by the implicit costs of testing for the ones that had to fail in order to bring the successful product to light. If it is true that the consumer benefit from drugs is already a large multiple of their retail price, there should be considerable room for that expansion. There are problems of unfair and therefore inefficient competition between grandfather products and new ones, but these would dissipate over the course of time. The public rather than the industry should be primarily concerned about the absorption of these rigorous testing costs and the delays that are inevitable in the introduction of new drugs, however efficacious, in a system that is designed to

assure that ineffective and unsafe ones have no chance of being permitted. I do
not agree with Professor Peltzman that the largest credible magnitude of a safety
defect in a drug is smaller than the benefits likely to accrue from the earlier
introduction of some life-saving wonder-drug. The potential for mischief from,
for example, another naphthylamine with a prolonged latent period is enormous.
So there is potentially a great problem of safety--the question is whether the testing procedures as <u>implemented</u> during the last decade have made a crucial contribution
to safety. Perhaps they have, more by disseminating a general sensitivity to the
safety issue than by the relevance of the specific procedures. Both the costs
and benefits of this atmosphere probably have more to do with deterrence, that is
non-introduction of products, than with the visible market.

Lately the FDA has given evidence of responsiveness to the issue of the life-
saving potential of a new introduction. And surely delays in optimal therapy owe
at least as much to the inadequacy of new drug information among doctors, to mal-
distribution of medical care, and to obstacles of basic research and its interface
with drug development than they do to FDA policies.

An important concern still is the evident degradation of morale in the research
groups of many drug companies under the impact of the regulatory procedures themselves, and perhaps even more of the public and political criticism that has been
directed at the industry. This problem of the social value placed on their services
can be epitomized in the price that a truly wonderful new drug, having to bear large
costs of development and of testing, might be expected to bring in the marketplace.
In principle why should not such a prescription be imagined to command as high a
price as brain surgery--assuming that the benefits of the drug and the general
competitive situation were in other respects comparable? Many drugs have been
marketed that had consumer benefits of this magnitude--most of the early antibiotics for example--but it is precisely the genius of American industry to have

been able to multiply the supply of such agents in a way that is simply not possible for competent brain surgeons. Only in the case of rather rare diseases would the price of the drug have to approach that of other aspects of medical care to return a profit that would recapture the costs of development. There are such markets where the number of potential consumers is relatively small, say in the thousands, and where it may nevertheless be necessary to invest many millions of dollars for their development. We must then ask, what is the political feasibility of a life-saving pill that costs $1,000?

I know that many drug companies simply cannot visualize finding themselves in a situation where they would, of course, be accused of being bloodsuckers if they demanded actual payment at these exorbitant levels. It would be safer not to get into such a political conflict to begin with! In some specific situations, groups of interested patients and their families might band together to help subsidize the costs of development either directly or by acting as political lobbies for government response. At such prices, government or other organized groups, such as insurance companies, are likely to bear much of the brunt of actual payment--they may still find it a good bargain--and some political clarity may still be achieved by more prior discussion of these principles. The dilemma is that everyone wants more safety and more efficacious drugs, but we have not quite agreed how this is to be paid for!

The problem of the $1,000 pill is, of course, a political one as well as a technical and economic one, and it may be further battered by being confused with some other problems of equality of access to health. There has been some discussion about consumer representation and what technical expertise this could bring to bear in decisions about policy. I think some of this may have partially missed the point. Technicians and scientists like myself are very hung up on efficiency. We would like to see the maximum gain for our investment. We would like to see an average increase in the overall health of the population. Taking a statistical and aggregated point of view, we have the broad vision to accept considerable variation in who will receive those benefits. Provided everybody benefits a little, we are willing to accept that some people may benefit a very great deal; at least rather that average gain than none at all. Not everyone thinks that way. It is certainly one of the axial conflicts of modern life that there are many who value equality of access to the care that is available and the equality of exposure to risk even higher than the absolute benefits. In effect, they would rather see everyone suffer the same ills and have equal access to the same gains, even at the expense of some share for everyone.

This is not something that can be or ought to be rationally decided, but we would be foolhardy not to recognize that this is an important aspect of our culture. It is one that politicians who have to be elected must understand very well. Some of the conflicts that we have heard about, I think, reflect inadequate understanding of the role of the two principles of equality and efficiency in contemporary life. It is the egalitarian point of view, more than any special technical expertise or even partisan consumer constituencies, that may have to be fairly represented in the development of further policy.

Finally, I would like to comment on the need to reconstruct our approach to safety testing. Generally we should be more concerned about regarding safety testing as a research problem and not as an obstacle course. You do not learn very much about the physiology of muscle contraction by setting up obstacles to see which drug can hurdle them and which cannot, and there is then very little generalization possible from one agent to the next in the way that testing is done today.

As we have escalated from a few millions to a few hundreds of millions of investment in this particular area, it seems to me a matter of great social urgency that these funds not be wasted in merely determining whether a particular agent is going to make it from a regulatory standpoint or not. The publication of the information that has been gleaned on a particular drug would, of course, be the first step. But this must go much further into the basic experimental design of determining what kinds of drugs are safe and what kinds of tests are going to elicit relevant information about them.

To do this will require a somewhat more broad-minded attitude and more discretionary power (yes, on the part of the FDA) in taking account of all available evidence, of demanding information about metabolism. Especially, they will have to give credit to information about related compounds which may have been very thoroughly worked over and where very rationally the substitution of an ethyl for a methyl group is extremely unlikely a priori to have very much impact on safety outcome. Not that you do not make some tests for it, but it is absurd to have to go through exactly the same routine in validating the safety of closely related derivatives of drugs that have been quite thoroughly tested as for totally new kinds of structures. I am not aware that this is part of regulatory policy at the present time.

In fact, there are any number of horror stories about drug companies that have contemplated the evolution of a product from an impure mixture to a pure compound, or reduced its dose, or discovered improved formulations involving the substitution of different salts, and have been deterred from bringing these innovations to the market. In spite of the fact that they have every inherent likelihood, even a certainty, of improving both the safety and the efficacy of the drug, the routine regulatory procedures believed to be required by the FDA are regarded as prohibitive. Perhaps these fears are fantasies or may be connected with some less obvious information that also bears on the utilities of these advances. If they are not fantasies then the FDA itself has a task of communication ahead of it. There is a story, however, that is not so apocryphal concerning certain soft lenses which must be labeled "safety in pregnancy has not been substantiated," a level of bureaucratic thinking that surely would deter the advancement of creative innovations. This kind of regulation may even be a satire intended to draw attention to the absurdities in the system. It would be funnier if we did not face enormous problems in determining the actual teratogenic and mutagenic hazards that probably do attach to a variety of products that have been on the market for some period of time.

DISCUSSION

KOSHLAND: The speech by Dr. Lederberg is now open for questioning. We will start with the Panel for Inquiry.

FRANKLIN A. LONG: I would like to ask a question concerning the graph that was sort of post-Kefauver in terms of the number of drugs introduced and their relative cost. Can one trust it because of the shortness of the time axis? My reason for asking this is that for commercial chemicals one company has analyzed rather carefully the time required for its products to begin to show acceptance, and the number is something like ten years. A product that ultimately turns out to have been quite successful can have a very slow takeoff and then sail up into high acceptance.

LEDERBERG: These are the numbers of introductions, not the market sales.

LONG: But it related to the question of whether the doctors thought these new drugs were any better than the old, and that, I take it, is a measure of acceptance. I would wonder whether there have been too few years post-Kefauver yet to say very much about that.

LEDERBERG: That is a legitimate point.

ROBERT McC. ADAMS: I have another question on the same graph. To what extent are we really looking at the rate of therapeutic innovation there? I guess my question could be phrased in another way. What is the definition of a new compound? It seems to me that one of the trends in the post-Kefauver period has been toward generic labeling, and I wonder whether that might not appear in this in some way, artificially reducing the --

LEDERBERG: Both pre- and post-Kefauver, these are new chemical entities, new single chemical entities.

95

ALLEN V. KNEESE: I should preface my statement by saying that I am an economist with an acute appreciation of the importance of the market as a resource allocative device. But your talk, Dr. Lederberg, almost convinced me that we ought to take the research, development, production, and distribution of drugs out of the private sector altogether.

It seems to me that there must be relatively few basic advances in drugs, but the kinds of market structure that exist in the industry provide a high incentive for what the economists refer to as product differentiation, the creation of nuances which can be sold with high-pressure advertising. This imposes a burden on testing. It imposes additional risks on the society. You have a very high discount rate in the industry, which is contrary to more basic research in the area, and I am just wondering what are the advantages of leaving the production and distribution of drugs in the private sector in the United States. Shouldn't we consider as a policy option simply taking it out of the private sector and putting it into the public sector?

LEDERBERG: I think you have the same problem with democracy. It is pretty awful, but what is any better? I think the history of efforts in this country to use central planning as the basis of capital allocation on a reasonably large scale is a rather sorry tale, and I do not know why one would expect it to be any better in the drug field. There are very large risks to be undertaken to be sure. We are speaking here not of the basic research, but of the choices and the allocation of capital resources for the purpose of developing an entity that might or might not make it later on in the market. The problem is whether one can really devise more satisfactory ways of making decisions other than rewarding those who seem to have done well and providing the negative incentive of bankruptcy or impoverishment to those who have not.

I think it deserves more consideration. But I think it is politically quite unrealistic to expect this to happen with drugs before it does in those many, many other industries which are much better candidates for this purpose.

KOSHLAND: Could I just explore this one minute? These comments enter an area which affects all basic research and applied research, namely, once the government takes over, do you subsidize research on a disease which affects .1 of 1 percent of the population, or do you have to work on diseases that affect over 20 percent? Must you work on the more prevalent disease first?

KNEESE: I was not necessarily proposing this very seriously. But it seemed to me that some of your implications, Dr. Lederberg, are clearly in that direction, and that there is a massive market failure.

LEDERBERG: I have some possible remedies that might be thought about. I think one ought to look at regulatory policies and their impact on cost of development more closely in relation to the size of the market for and of the public exposure to a given product than I think is formally done at the present time. I am sure this is done informally on a very large scale. To demand $10 million worth of testing on a drug whose social risk and social utility may be less than that may be quite unreasonable. I am not sure that all of the apparatus is legislatively available to enable one to make discriminations of that kind. But plainly there ought to be waivers of some sort for drugs of very limited market.

On the other hand, one could imagine the potential consumers of specialized drugs pooling their resources and influence. I do not see a great political problem in what you referred to, Dr. Koshland. We have institutes of the NIH that cover a very wide range of diseases, some of them very rare, some of them very general. And that, at the more basic level, certainly works out very well.

98

I do not know all the reasons why central planning of investment has worked so badly. I could make a lot of guesses about it, given other aspects of our political process, but "rivers and harbors" might be a very good sort of general allegation for what is likely to happen. How much better or worse that would be than the present system I think is worth investigating.

RICHARD L. HALL: Earlier there seemed to be at least a minimal degree of dissatisfaction with the way in which these products have been regulated. I find it interesting that we now are considering that the agencies with whose actions there is dissatisfaction in regulating might be asked to produce as well.

(Laughter)

LEDERBERG: That is totally irrelevant. I mean sometimes you put the right people in the wrong role and they will do what you might expect. I think that is very much an open question.

What I am very much concerned about is that health is such a potent source of ideological controversy that it is very, very difficult to get efficient allocative mechanisms operating there. We very often find the profit making mechanism under severe attack ex post facto, and that, of course, is what would be wrong with a $1,000 pill. The amortization of research and development might have cost that $1,000, and it might cost $.50 to produce. The pill might be "pirated" in Italy and then imported under a generic name. There would be all kinds of pressures against profiteering by the drug industry in those circumstances. It is very difficult to sustain a position in favor of depriving the poor of that costly pill. And others would complain about subsidizing their purchase, although this would be analogous to paying a surgeon's fees under Medicare. I do not think there is a clear general understanding of the economic foundations that are needed for these developments.

I would deplore half-baked efforts to socialize the drug industry. I would much rather it went the whole way and gave us a viable mechanism than to have it pulled apart from both sides and left in shambles. I do not think it is quite a shambles. I do not think we have seen really convincing data that drugs are impossible to invest in and impossible to produce. I do not have enough information about the shrewdness of the strategies that the more successful companies have been able to implement. I hope we will hear more about that. But there certainly are efforts that are intended to have this half-baked consequence of tearing down the private enterprise without having built a viable alternative.

PHILIP MORRISON: What are the steps in market limitation now followed? Evidently the expectations depend on the allowable market size. I expect now that there is a jump from an experimental use with highly specific licensing to the time a drug is fully accepted. Are there intermediate steps? Could you license a million doses, ten, whatever? Would that not be another means?

LEDERBERG: I think Peter Hutt may have that on his agenda for later discussion. But it would certainly be one of my explicit proposals, especially for what I might call the mega drugs, which have been talked about as prospects. I am not sure there are any real examples at the present time. But people would be concerned about the possibility of development of new kinds of contraceptives, say male contraceptives, or of atherosclerosis-preventing agents. There are a number of dreams one might have for agents that would be on the boundary, you might say, of being nutrients and of being drugs which might be used over very, very long periods and would have immense markets.

Now there is simply no amount of anticipatory testing, either in animals or in controlled clinical trials, that is able to provide the assurance that one is going to demand for a market exposure of that size. It would seem to me, particularly in that arena, that it would be very advisable to contemplate having intermediate levels of introduction. This would allow specially qualified practitioners to operate under a definite mandate to report adverse response, and to work in a fashion that gives them the best chance to pick up adverse responses. Once an agent has been introduced to the entire population, your epidemiology goes to pot. If there are clearly defined segments, then you have a better chance of seeing differentials in health response that might then be the consequence of this new agent.

Each of these huge project ventures, however, will have to be looked at ad hoc. They will all have their own very special characteristics. Until we have a really tangible example that is ready to go to the line with respect to the large-scale investments, it may be a little bit pointless to try to articulate a detailed policy to further their development. But that a policy will be entertained, that there will be special responses for programs that might entail investments in the hundreds of millions of dollars, markets of billions, and consumer exposures of tens or hundreds of millions of people -- it might well be important to open up that discussion right now.

MORRISON: It seems to me, even on a less serious level, the introduction of drugs which are not aimed at major therapy -- the famous, terrible example of which is thalidomide -- that drugs which have no intense therapeutic demand or are not life saving might be introduced by stepped procedures which would only defer the return and would very much increase the public safety.

LEDERBERG: I would certainly agree, if only to increase the chance of picking up the response from an epidemiological standpoint. But then you are going to face the following political dilemma. If you make this available, so to speak, only to the rich or the well qualified, you are depriving the poor. If you make it available to the poor, you are using them as guinea pigs for an untried drug. It is very hard to find a way out of this dilemma.

KOSHLAND: There is always the middle class.

LEDERBERG: Maybe we need not only more basic knowledge on the one side, but a more stable social structure. I think as long as we are as riven as we have been in the last five or ten years and have such an intense adversary culture, these problems may be politically unresolvable.

I would like to make one final point. The drug companies may well say, "Why pick on us?" I have heard a few remarks like that, and I would agree that there are many, many other hazards that are at least commensurate with the risks in proportion to the benefits that patients get at the hands of drugs. I think drugs have received from a certain point of view an inordinate amount of attention with respect to their risks. I am perfectly confident that we will find common foodstuffs -- spices, cheeses, whatnot -- which have exotic chemicals in them that will be proved to be very serious chronic health hazards. So, why pick on drugs? I think drugs are the pathfinders. They have a very explicit and a very visible target in terms of the people who can be forced to invest in risk finding research of this kind. It would be much more difficult to get the licorice manufacturer to get very much concerned about what is really a very serious toxicological problem. One of my friends nearly died of aldosteronism when he unwisely consumed about a pound of licorice in one week, to give an example. I do not think that is within the purview of the FDA.

The drug industry can be the technological pathfinder, but I will say that it is rapidly getting an awful lot of company. At least it will not feel lonely in the very near future in being concerned about making these kinds of investments on a large scale.

KOSHLAND: We are not going to let you off for the day, Dr. Lederberg, because many of the things you brought out will be relevant to the talks and discussion to follow. Thank you very much.

ACADEMY FORUM: PART II

JOHN R. HOGNESS, M.D.
      CHAIRMAN

JOHN R. HOGNESS: It seemed to me, as I listened to some of the comments by our speakers, particularly the first two, that there was some sense of criticism of the scientist and the physician on the one hand, and some sense of perhaps implied denigration of the consumer on the other hand. I am sure that these were not intended to be severe criticisms. More interesting, however, was the fact that each group wanted to claim the mantle of the other. As a result, we had providers wanting to be consumers and, to a more limited degree, consumers feeling that they were in some way reacting to scientific aspects of problems.

This is all by way of introducing a story about the Pope who died and went up to Heaven. At the Pearly Gates there was a long, long line of people waiting for registration, vaccination, and so forth. Assuming that his title and history would afford him some priority, the Pope went up to the head of the line. There he was informed that this was a democracy and, unfortunately from his point of view but fortunately from the point of view of all other consumers, that he would have to wait his turn. Just as the Pope returned to the end of the line, a man in a white coat with a stethoscope dangling from his pocket scurried up to the front of the line and was immediately ushered through the Pearly Gates. The Pope was incensed. He ran forward and said, "I thought that this was a democracy." "Shh," he was told. "That was God. Every once in a while he likes to play doctor."

I am not sure of the moral of this story. It doubtlessly is open to a variety of interpretations, and you are at liberty to choose your own.

We now will turn to two other aspects of the complexities surrounding the design of policy on drugs and food additives. These presentations will be followed by interrogation by the other speakers, the panel, and members of the audience.

Oliver H. Lowry is chairman of the Department of Pharmacology in the School of Medicine, Washington University. Dr. Lowry will discuss a scientist's viewpoint.

Peter Barton Hutt, assistant general counsel for the Food and Drug Division of the Department of Health, Education, and Welfare, is well-qualified to present the viewpoint of a regulator.

A Scientist's Viewpoint

Oliver H. Lowry, M.D.

The dangers associated with drugs are of two kinds: dangers inherent in the drug itself, and dangers from misuse of the drug. I will restrict myself to the inherent dangers from drugs when properly used, even though the greatest dangers by far today are from the improper use of the drugs we have.

There can be no question, I think, about the central role of science in detecting dangers in drugs and in discovering ways to increase drug safety. The value as well as the dangers of a drug can only be determined by objective testing, that is to say, by scientific evaluation. There is no other way. Attitudes about drugs are especially susceptible to myth and superstition. It is well known that what a doctor thinks and tells his patient about a drug can influence the effects of that drug. Judging from my own friends, most laymen have one or more erroneous ideas about preventing and curing disease. Doctors themselves, down through the ages, usually did more harm than good because there were no hard therapeutic facts about their alleged remedies. Many a king has been hastened to his grave by his well-meaning physicians.

Since those old days, things have changed for the better as the result of objective, scientific study. One of the first things that resulted from a really hard look was that most old-time drugs were found to be junk and were discarded. Then there followed, as you know, in the best medical circles what was almost a no-drug period, a period, as has been said, of therapeutic nihilism. After this, a new start was made. Over the past forty years truly effective and relatively safe drugs have been developed. Science has brought this about. From now on we must seek ways to bring science to bear in the most effective

manner on drug safety problems as well as on the development of better drugs,
never forgetting that we are a long way from effective treatment for some of our
worst diseases.

There is one very large problem which every professional or layman concerned
about drugs must take into account: The human machine is almost unbelievably complicated. This means that the actions of drugs to tamper with this machine are
certain to be very complicated. The machine already appeared exceedingly complex
in 1938 when the Food, Drug, and Cosmetic Act was enacted. In the thirty-five
years since then, science has accumulated a fantastic amount of information about
the living machine. In so doing, we have learned that our machinery is actually
far more complicated than anyone had realized, and today we are obviously still
nowhere near a complete understanding of how the human machine works.

Drugs are simply chemical compounds which react with that machinery, hopefully to make it work better. Therefore, we are a long way from a full understanding of drug actions and drug dangers. Sometimes, in trying to repair our
machinery with drugs, we seem to be only a little bit better off than the man who
succeeds in fixing his television set by giving it a kick. One deceptive thing
is that the body does not look all that complicated. I have a headache. I take
a pill of a simple compound, aspirin, and the headache goes away. What is so complicated about that? I assure you that the process is very complicated and not
understood at all until the last year or two. Part of the action of aspirin now
appears to be due to blocking the synthesis of a group of normal regulator substances which were only recently discovered by basic scientists.

My view is that this complexity of the human body and the complexity of its
reactions with drugs, plus our own incomplete knowledge, must to a very large
extent determine what would be optimal policy on drugs and food additives.

Considering our ignorance, we have in fact been remarkably successful in using drugs to protect, to repair, and to alter human machinery. Although we are all aware of the ill effects and dangers with many existing drugs, these side effects are minor compared to the great benefits from these drugs. I doubt that, given the present state of knowledge about living things, we could have expected a much better ratio of good to bad effects, no matter what laws had been passed or how they had been implemented. Nevertheless, although we may be reasonably satisfied with past performance, we must not be satisfied to let it rest there. We must correct deficiencies of present drug classes, and we must find remedies for the many diseases for which no remedies exist.

Given our lack of knowledge, one of the things we must clearly do is to encourage basic research on the living machine itself and how it interacts with drugs. There are those who say that we have acquired enough knowledge and, therefore, let us now get on with the job of applying that knowledge to human problems. This is a recommendation that can only arise from a profound misunderstanding of the human organism. The very recent discouragement of support for basic science can only delay the development of safe, effective drugs. Except for this unfortunate trend, which I trust is temporary, I view the situation as very good for the future. As science has learned more about the living machine, it has acquired powerful tools for studying the reactions between drugs and that machine. Let me give one example.

Most drugs are converted by the body into one or more metabolic products which may be beneficial or harmful or simply innocuous. One of the reasons why testing a drug on experimental animals is not sufficient is that man may convert the drug into different products than those of the particular experimental animals used. Because it is possible that one of these metabolic products produced by man alone might be harmful, it is important to determine the metabolic fate of each drug in man himself.

Thirty-five years ago the study of drug metabolism was slow and cumbersome and inadequate. Today, on the other hand, there are laboratory tools and techniques which permit the metabolism of a drug to be determined rapidly and accurately even with small, harmless test dosages in human beings. If, as a result of such tests, a unique metabolite of a drug is discovered in man, that compound can be tested in experimental animals for its possible toxicity. This is only one illustration of the fact that science now has increasingly better ways to study drugs. There are many others that could be cited.

However, we are still a long way from knowing enough about the body to understand the mechanism of many drug reactions and of many of the unpleasant or dangerous side effects. It is going to take a lot of imaginative basic research to dig these things out. Simple, blind empirical testing of drugs is certainly not enough.

A major consideration is how we can do better in regard to safety without stifling the development of new and improved drugs. We have always been faced with two opposite dangers: undertesting of drugs, which leaves too much risk of toxicity; and overtesting, which creates the certainty of greater suffering from disease because of undue delay in introduction of an important drug.

For example, there are those who believe that the Salk polio vaccine was introduced prematurely. The delay of two or three years might have prevented the Cutter incident. On the other hand, it is almost a certainty that a two- or three-year delay in the introduction of the Salk vaccine would have resulted in 100,000 cases, or more, of paralytic poliomyelitis. It was known ahead of time that this was true, and the risk was taken deliberately. Against this 100,000 sure cases of poliomyelitis, there were some 260 cases which developed as the result of improperly manufactured vaccine, a ratio of 400 to 1. The benefit was rightly judged to far exceed the risk.

As an opposite example, the benefit to be gained from having one more sedative drug did not, in my estimation, justify the risk of introducing thalidomide without far more exhaustive testing than it had received. To make decisions in regard to benefit versus risk is often very difficult. It would seem wise if the FDA had available the best advice in the country in many of these decisions.

There is another consideration which also leads to the conclusion that there may be need for better ways of providing advice from scientists outside as well as inside government and industry. This arises as another important consequence of this exquisite complexity of the body and of its interactions with drugs. It is impossible for one person and difficult for a small group to have the wide range of knowledge necessary to assess adequately the procedures by which different types of drugs and food additives are tested, or should be tested, and evaluated.

Most of us have been impressed by the outstanding success of another review system. Under the peer review system of the National Institutes of Health, active investigators in different fields of biomedical research from all over the country provide a breadth of expert review that would be impossible by the NIH itself on an in-house basis. This peer review system has proved to be an almost ideal way of getting the greatest public value out of federal support with a minimum of bureaucratic problems. I would strongly urge that by some analogous system greater advantage be taken of the scientific expertise of this country as a whole in the review of new drug applications, in the appraisal of existing drugs, and in determining where basic research studies are most needed.

The NIH study section system would not be directly convertible for the purposes of drug evaluations. There are too many differences between the research grant situation and that of new drug evaluations. Nevertheless, the basic approach could be similar. Without wanting to be too specific, without claiming original- ity, and certainly without claiming that something of this sort is not already in process, let me suggest the following. There could be a roster of scientific ad- visors selected from the country over, chiefly from outside government but also including many from the FDA, from the NIH, and so on. This roster would include those directly knowledgeable about drugs and about clinical applications plus (and I think this very important) at least as many other basic investigators from a broad spectrum of biomedical science. From this roster, advisory panels could be set up for each new major drug application. Or, what I believe would be prefer- able, standing advisory panels could be organized, each with special expertise in a particular field. It has been pointed out that there would be a great value in having advice from such groups about a test program prior to its initiation and during each of its phases, as well as appraisal of the results after its comple- tion.

The panels would advise about whether shortcuts are desirable or whether addi- tional tests are needed. Such panels also could advise on the most important and difficult question of whether the potential value of a new drug justifies the risks involved in its introduction. Advice from the panels could improve the individual testing programs and then allow the FDA to make final decisions with greater assurance. Regardless of the uncertainty about how well the risks from a new drug can be evaluated, I submit that a broad spectrum group of advisors would be in a better position to apply judgment on this score than a narrower, strictly drug knowledgeable group.

I believe one of the most useful and significant contributions of such broadly based panels would be in regard to the difficult ethical questions that arise in connection with drug testing in man. Unless medical progress is to cease and safety is to be ignored, drug testing on human beings must go on. It is clear that in such testing, ethical decisions must be made with the benefit of the best scientific advice and, of course, the best ethical advice from those who are competent to give it.

Each human testing case needs to be decided on its own merits. It is one thing to decide if it is proper to persuade a healthy volunteer to take small amounts of an anti-hypertensive drug that has been carefully tested in animals. It is quite another thing to decide on the ethics of the testing in man of an anti-cancer agent which it is hoped will kill cancer cells without killing too many normal cells. It is perhaps possible to draw up general ethical guidelines for drug testing in man, but I believe the application of such guidelines to specific cases cannot be wisely made without the fullest possible scientific information and the broadest unbiased advice.

In addition to responsibilities for new major drug applications, the panels could also, from time to time, be given assignments to review accepted drugs and drug uses. This has been done in the past and is still being done, but it could be extended beyond what is possible at the present time with ad hoc advisory groups. The difference is that the panels would be permanent, with rotation according to a suitable schedule, and would include persons with a much broader breadth of scientific knowledge about man as a whole.

Two other important jobs could be performed by these panels. One is to suggest specific areas where more drug research is needed. The other is to spell out where better drug therapy is needed and where it is realistic to believe that better therapy might be developed.

An important part of such an advisory system, I believe, would be a national food and drug advisory council analogous to the national advisory councils of the NIH. To this council the panels would report at least some of their major decisions. The council could enter into the more important problems and make recommendations for research support and for long-range policy changes. Taken all together, I submit that such an advisory system would be of great value to the drug companies, to the FDA, and (more important than either of these) to the public as a whole.

Two difficulties with such a system have been pointed out to me. The first is that the secrecy regarded as necessary, at least during the early stages of drug testing, would be a problem. I cannot believe that the secrecy problem is insurmountable. The panels might not be activated until after initial testing, by which time essential information about the drug would have to become rather widely disseminated in any event.

The second difficulty is that of conflict of interest. Many of those senior scientists who are knowledgeable about drugs serve as consultants for one or another drug company. This also, I believe, can be handled. There are actually a great many younger investigators to draw upon, some of them perhaps wiser than their elders. Conflict of interest would be no problem with many of the basic investigators who are not primarily working with drugs, but who would be the invaluable broad spectrum members of the advisory panels.

Let me review several points in summary:

- The human body and the interaction of drugs with it are so complicated and so incompletely understood that no one can yet predict ahead of time what dangers there may be from a new drug or a new application of a drug.

- This complexity and lack of knowledge indicate that a semiempirical approach to drug safety is still necessary.

- Past experience with drugs, plus progressive improvements in the way to study interaction of drugs with the body, can greatly improve and speed up this semiempirical drug testing process.

- Until the human body is much better understood than at present, there will always be the possibility that a new drug, in spite of apparently adequate testing, may ultimately cause a small degree of harm to many people or a large degree of harm to a few people. Judgment as to potential benefit and possible risk from a new drug is often very difficult and should be made on the basis of the best scientific advice. The same is true of the ethical problems arising out of the need to test new drugs on human beings.

- With these considerations in mind, in order to achieve for the public maximum drug safety on the one hand and maximum benefits from drugs on the other, it is recommended that basic research be strongly encouraged and in no way sacrificed for more obvious immediate health goals. It also is recommended that an advisory system to the FDA be set up which would include a wide spectrum of basic biomedical scientists and clinical scientists from both inside and outside of government.

A Regulator's Viewpoint

Peter Barton Hutt

Regulation of the safety of food and drugs should be an extremely simple and perfunctory task. After all, one need only hold up the indisputable scientific facts, and compare them with equally explicit statutory requirements. The regulatory result will then ineluctably follow, with the full concurrence and acclaim of the Congress, the regulated industry, the consumer advocates, the academic community, and the public at large.

Unfortunately, however, this does not occur in the real world. In the twenty months that I have held my current position, I cannot recall one major safety decision by the Food and Drug Administration -- regardless which way it was decided -- that has failed to provoke prolonged, and at times bitter, public dispute. Moreover, even if we had reached exactly the opposite conclusion on any of those decisions, it is unlikely that there would have been any greater or lesser amount of dispute.

In short, public policy design and execution with respect to the safety of food and drugs is highly, and perhaps irretrievably, controversial. It raises up a welter of subjective and emotional views that often obscure rational analysis and that can severely hinder regulation by scientific decision making.

My remarks will initially outline the statutory mandate for safe food and drugs. I will then discuss what I discern to be the principal obstacles to decision making on safety issues. Finally, I will describe the action that is being taken to improve this situation.

I

Any discussion of decision making on the safety of food and drugs must begin with an understanding of the broad statutory mandate Congress has given to the Food and Drug Administration.

As early as the Food and Drugs Act of 1906, Congress demanded protection of the public from unsafe food and drugs. That law prohibited the use in food of "any added poisonous or other added deleterious ingredient which may render such article injurious to health." It similarly prohibited the use in drugs of any "ingredient deleterious or detrimental to health."

When Congress modernized this law in 1938, it was unable to improve upon those general statutory admonitions. The Federal Food, Drug, and Cosmetic Act states that a food may not contain any "poisonous or deleterious substance which may render it injurious to health," and that a drug may not be recommended for any use for which it is "dangerous to health." Even the Food Additives Amendment of 1958 and the more recent Drug Amendments of 1962, which were enacted specifically to provide more stringent protection against unsafe food and drugs, again are couched in very broad and general terms. The food additive provisions of the law require the Food and Drug Administration to consider "safety factors which in the opinion of experts qualified by scientific training and experience to evaluate the safety of food additives are generally recognized as appropriate for the use of animal experimentation data." The new drug provisions of the law state simply that safety must be shown by "adequate tests by all methods reasonably applicable to show whether or not such drug is safe for use."

The only detailed safety criteria contained in the statute are in the famous anti-cancer clauses which have been a source of great discussion today. In contrast to the public attention they have received, however, those clauses are actually an issue in very few safety decisions made by the Food and Drug Admin-

istration -- certainly far less than one-tenth of one percent of those decisions.

In most of the instances where they have been an issue, the matter has been resolved

by using sound scientific judgment, based on general principles of food safety,

before it was necessary to even consider invoking them. The so-called Delaney

clause has been invoked specifically on only two occasions, neither of which was

the widely publicized banning of cyclamates or DES. As a practical matter, there-

fore, the anti-cancer clauses are a relatively insignificant factor in the daily

administration of the safety provisions of the law, although they unquestionably

present a fascinating subject for discussion at a forum such as this one.

In giving the Food and Drug Administration sweeping authority to require that

all food and drugs be safe, therefore, Congress has relied upon a very broad and

general mandate rather than upon narrow and specific rules. Not one of the cri-

tical statutory terms or phrases which control the numerous safety decisions made

daily by the Food and Drug Administration is anywhere defined in the statute. Nor,

indeed, do I believe that they can or should be defined at this point in time.

Safety evaluation is today an imprecise and uncertain task. Until the ambiguities

and imponderables that now inhere in that task are clarified and elucidated, rigid

safety definitions seem unlikely to lead to sound public policy.

Perhaps the best example of the thicket into which any legislative body wanders

in attempting to enact any rigid safety criteria may be found in the various anti-

cancer clauses now contained in the Act. Regardless whether one supports or

opposes inclusion of a specific anti-cancer provision in the law -- and I emphasize

that I take no position whatever on that issue -- I think that we can all agree that

the present versions are indefensible from any viewpoint.

In 1958, when it first included an anti-cancer clause in the law, Congress

applied it only to good ingredients that are not generally recognized as safe or

were not previously approved for use in food by the Food and Drug Administration
or the United States Department of Agriculture. From this, one might deduce that
Congress favored use of old and familiar carcinogens over newly discovered ones.

In 1960, a second anti-cancer clause was enacted as part of the Color Additive Amendments. This time Congress applied the clause to colors that are per-
manently approved for use in food and drugs after adequate safety testing, but not
to colors that are only temporarily or provisionally allowed for such use because
of a lack of adequate safety testing. From this, one might deduce that Congress
thought that the American public was entitled to at least a few more colorful
years of some of its favorite carcinogens before it must face the prospect of a
supply of very drab food and drugs.

Then in 1962, faced with the inconsistency of its distinction between pre-
1958 and post-1958 carcinogens, Congress amended the two clauses to solve the problem. The principal issue in 1962, as you may know, was the use of diethylstilbestrol (DES), which had been approved for use by some manufacturers as an animal
growth promotant prior to 1958. Those manufacturers who had a pre-1958 approval
could continue to make it, and all others could not. Instead of eliminating this
distinction, however, Congress added yet another in order to require the Food
and Drug Administration to allow production of DES by all manufacturers. Under
the Drug Amendments of 1962 -- and subsequently in the Animal Drug Amendments of
1968 -- the Food and Drug Administration must now approve a known carcinogen for
use in food-producing animals as long as available analytical methodology is
unable to detect that carcinogen in the food obtained from the animal. From this,
one might deduce that Congress simply wanted to inject a little excitement into
an otherwise rather stodgy law, and reverted to that favorite old childhood game
of hide-and-seek.

Nor is that the last chapter. In 1972, when scientists finally did find DES in animal livers by using radioactive tracers, and the Food and Drug Administration banned it from animal feed with a five-month phaseout period, the Senate promptly passed a bill to ban use of DES immediately. The House did not act on that bill. From this, one might deduce that half of Congress sincerely regretted that it had ever wandered into this thicket, and the other half was simply immobilized by the total incongruity of what had happened.

This rather incredible chronicle of legislative groping for political and scientific truth holds important lessons for all of us. Congress, in attempting to deal in detail with just one of many thousands of safety issues, has clearly floundered. The rule it has erected is so riddled with exemptions, exceptions, and loopholes as to make it indefensible in its present form. Again, I take no position on any possible other clauses. It presently serves more as a barrier to removing unsafe animal drugs from the market than as a measure for public protection. Indeed, that is the very reason why it is so seldom invoked. Its underlying purpose is, and properly should be, served by the general safety provisions of the law.

In the last analysis, regulation of the safety of food and drugs must depend upon informed scientific judgment. The scientific uncertainties that exist at this moment in history simply require that safety determinations be made more on the basis of subjective evaluation than objective standards. And so long as this remains the situation, it must be expected that reasonable men can, and frequently will, differ on the judgment made by the Food and Drug Administration in any given situation, and thus on whether the statutory requirement of safety is properly being implemented in that particular situation.

II

The Food and Drug Administration's decision making process on safety issues, and the public perception of it, are hampered by five basic obstacles. No one of these obstacles is critical, but their combined impact can at times be quite severe. While each may be present to a greater or lesser degree in any particular safety decision, there is probably no major safety decision involving the Food and Drug Administration to which all do not contribute. Let me enumerate them.

First, the scientific data base is seldom adequate to make a definitive safety judgment on any food or drug.

With every passing year, scientists develop new, more sophisticated safety testing methodology. Just one adverse finding, from whatever test method employed, seems sufficient today to call into public question the safety of virtually any ingredient used in food or drugs. If the product has been on the market for many years, as is true with much of our food supply, it is unlikely that it would have been subjected to many, if indeed any, of the scientific tests that are considered commonplace today. It simply is not feasible, as we all well know, every year to go back and retest, using the latest methodology, all the components of food and drugs that previously have been placed on the market. And even with the most recent additions to the marketplace, it is doubtful that any substance has been, or can be, so thoroughly tested as to preclude further scientific question.

It has long been recognized that no amount of human or animal testing can ever demonstrate the absolute absence of harm. All that one can ever show with certainty is the existence of harm. The marketing of any product therefore carries with it an inescapable but undeterminable risk. With the recent association of vaginal cancer in the female offspring of mothers using diethylstilbestrol during pregnancy, moreover, this point has become a matter of immediate and serious policy concern to the Food and Drug Administration. We presently have no way whatever to predict this type of future harm for products about to be marketed, and our ability to monitor the safety of already marketed products is similarly limited. Even centuries of use of natural substances in the diet, without noticeable adverse effects, cannot be regarded as proof of safety since it is based only upon uncontrolled observations.

Thus, proof of complete safety appears at this moment to be an illusory goal. Both those who challenge and those who defend the safety of any particular substance can do so with the assurance that information adequate either to support or to refute their contentions is not now available, and may never be. And today's decisions on the safety of food and drugs will therefore inevitably be made on the basis of incomplete scientific information.

Second, even when substantial safety data are available on a particular substance, there is seldom scientific agreement on the meaning or significance of that information.

Scientists have been far more successful in inventing new methods of safety testing than they have been in determining the significance of the results obtained. This is particularly true with the still evolving animal tests for carcinogenicity, teratogenicity, and mutagenicity. The meaning of adverse results obtained from these experiments, and especially their relevance to human use, is usually open to severe scientific disagreement. And of course the likelihood of obtaining at least one adverse or questionable finding increases with every test that is conducted.

Even those animal tests which have been widely accepted by scientists frequently produce results that are variable and inconclusive. Every scientist knows that quite different results can be obtained from a standard test protocol using

different animal species, different strains of the same species, different animal
rations, different routes of administration, and a host of far more subtle variables. Different laboratories not infrequently obtain diverse results even trying
to replicate the identical testing procedures.

In short, the significance of much of the animal safety testing conducted
today is poorly understood, and the widely variable results obtained are subject
to differing interpretations. Its usefulness in the design and execution of sound
public policy under these circumstances is unfortunately limited. As a matter of
practical necessity, therefore, we often regulate more out of fear of the unknown
than out of respect and appreciation of the known. And until science begins to
bring greater understanding to safety testing, regulation of the safety of food
and drugs must be accomplished in the midst of unresolvable scientific disagreement.

Third, even assuming that an adequate scientific data base were available, together with scientific agreement on the meaning and significance of the data, there
appears to be no public or scientific consensus today on the risk or uncertainty
acceptable to justify the marketing of any substance as a food or drug.

To some, who favor a return to more simple days, no risk or uncertainty whatever is justified for any addition of a chemical to food. They would, indeed,
require a showing of some greater benefit to society before any such ingredient is
permitted. To others, who see enormous progress in food technology and nutrition
from the use of food additives, the usual risks associated with technological innovation are regarded as entirely reasonable. Even in the area of therapeutic drugs,
there is intense public dispute about whether, to use one example, the risks of
an abortion outweigh the risks that are raised by the use of DES as a postcoital
contraceptive.

We must recognize that this type of issue presents fundamental differences in philosophical principles, not simply a narrow dispute on technical details. It raises the most basic questions of personal beliefs and human values -- the degree of risk or uncertainty that any individual is willing to accept in his daily life. Attempts to resolve such an issue on the basis of rigorous scientific testing or analytical discourse therefore simply miss the point. A mathematical benefit-risk formula or computer program may eventually be able to quantitate the risk or uncertainty that inheres in a given product, but it is not even relevant to the moral and ethical issues involved in deciding whether this degree of risk or uncertainty is acceptable.

This problem arises whenever new doubts or suspicions are cast upon the safety of an already marketed substance. Those who favor a very low public risk demand that the product immediately be removed from the market. Those who advocate a higher risk demand that it remain on the market until it is shown to be unsafe. If, as I suspect will happen, we eventually prove that many of our basic foods and drugs contain at least trace amounts of highly toxic substances -- including carcinogens, teratogens, and mutagens -- the public simply will have to face these issues in a more forthright way that it has up to now.

One does not need a degree in science to hold and express deeply felt beliefs on the degree of risk or uncertainty society should accept from food and drugs. Nor, indeed, does a scientific background equip anyone with any greater insight into the intricacies of this type of policy issue or any more impressive credentials or greater authority to act as an arbiter in resolving these matters. As long as we remain a free society, these basic philosophical principles will, and properly should, remain the subject of intense public scrutiny and debate.

Fourth, there is enormous and continuing public pressure for the Food and Drug Administration to resolve whatever may be the latest current safety issue promptly and decisively.

Delay and indecision weaken public confidence and intensify fear and concern. Industrial representatives, faced with potential harm to their economic interests, demand reassurance that the public need fear no danger. Consumer activists, sensing a further victory in their war against unsafe products, intensify the public campaign to discredit the suspect product. Members of Congress, reacting to the legitimate concern of their constituencies, demand a prompt resolution. The media, recognizing a story of interest to the entire public, do not fail to give it ample prominence. Thus, regardless of the uncertainties and imponderables, a decision must frequently be reached immediately on the basis of whatever meager information may exist.

On economic issues, a government agency may be able to take its time, to sift the facts, to make further investigations, and to act calmly and deliberately. Certainly, scientists in the academic world have ample opportunity to conduct further studies, obtain additional information, and engage in reflective thought before reaching difficult judgments on complex scientific issues. In the emotion charged atmosphere of a botulism or cancer scare, however, that process is necessarily foreshortened. It is simply unrealistic to believe that the Food and Drug Administration can ignore, or even long resist, the need to act promptly and decisively under those circumstances.

Fifth, regardless of the outcome of the decision, those who disagree with it will continue to pursue the matter through all available channels, while those who agree with it will inevitably remain silent, preparing themselves for the next issue.

Graceful acceptance, or even grudging acquiescence, by those who have lost any important safety decision is a rare exception. And praise or even mild support from those who have prevailed is equally rare.

The price of virtually any major safety decision is at least one congressional hearing, and perhaps more -- regardless which way the decision goes. At least one congressman will be persuaded, sooner or later, that important facts were not adequately considered, or appropriate weight was not given to particular viewpoints, and therefore that the entire matter should be subjected to further public scrutiny. This is obviously an important and appropriate congressional function.

For those in industry or consumer organizations whose views were not accepted by the Food and Drug Administration, moreover, there is ready access to the courts. This is not only their right, but indeed their duty when they believe we have made an incorrect decision or acted unlawfully. Quite frequently, the economic stakes are extremely high. I have framed a law that, while not immutable, certainly has general application today: Industry is likely to challenge in the courts any Food and Drug Administration action where the net adverse economic impact exceeds the legal fees involved.

Thus, no matter how promptly and decisively the matter is resolved, it usually does not end there. It continues to reverberate in the media, in Congress, in the courts, and in public debate for months or years to come. Invariably, new scientific evidence will come to light on which one side of the issue or the other will find new sustenance. It is not at all surprising, therefore, that the 1959 cranberry episode, the 1962 thalidomide tragedy, and the 1969 cyclamate ban are still discussed as though they happened last week. I am confident that our current ban of DES as an animal growth promotant, and whatever decision we ultimately reach on saccharin, will still be debated in lively terms twenty years hence. Nor is there any greater likelihood that a scientific or policy consensus on these issues will ultimately be reached then than there is that one can be reached at this moment.

As a lawyer, I am not only accustomed to the adversary process, but also am a very strong advocate of it. Nevertheless, we must be careful to prevent trial by combat from replacing reasoned decision making on important safety issues.

III

In the midst of all this disarray and confusion stands the Food and Drug Administration, bearing its heavy statutory responsibility of assuring the safety of all food and drugs marketed in this country. With inadequate scientific data, with fundamental scientific disagreement on technical issues and public disagreement on policy issues, with the necessity to act decisively and promptly, and with the assurance of widespread dispute about whatever action emerges, the Food and Drug Administration daily makes some of the most important public policy decisions that directly affect all of our lives. I say this with neither exaggeration nor rancor, but simply with candor based upon daily experience and active participation in this process. Nor do I believe that it is reasonable to expect that these very real obstacles will change dramatically, much less disappear, in the near future.

These obstacles have clearly taken their toll. Public and congressional confidence in the ability of the Food and Drug Administration to carry out its statutory responsibilities unquestionably has been undermined. It thus has become apparent that the Food and Drug Administration must meet this challenge or face potential destruction.

Instead of throwing up our hands in despair, however, we have already instituted major changes in the decision making processes of the Food and Drug Administration to accommodate and even to assimilate these obstacles. Faced with deeper public concern about the safety of food and drugs than ever before, we have begun

to open up the Food and Drug Administration's deliberations to substantially greater public scrutiny and participation, and thus equally greater public accountability
than perhaps any government agency in history. These changes, which are still in
progress and will undoubtedly not be completed for some time, involve three essential elements.

First, we are developing new procedural mechanisms to guarantee that all interested persons have access to the Food and Drug Administration before important
decisions are made. These procedures cannot permit decisions to be tied up forever
in needless red tape that only delays the process. But they must provide all segments of the public -- consumer activists, the regulated industry, the academic
world, and the public at large -- information about what the Food and Drug Administration is considering and a meaningful opportunity for their voices to be heard
before a decision is reached.

We have, in the past eighteen months, developed such procedures for review of
over-the-counter drugs and biological products. Anyone may submit written information or may make oral presentations to the reviewing panel at its frequent meetings. Our new procedures which for the first time permit the Food and Drug Administration to impose additional safety testing for already marketed food ingredients encourage petitions by any person who wishes to designate specific testing that should be required for a particular substance. We have just announced
a public hearing to consider internal guidelines that will govern the formulation
and labeling of a class of prescription drugs -- the first such hearing in the Food
and Drug Administration's history. These are just a few examples of the changes
taking place. And we are now beginning to rethink all of the procedures by which
the Food and Drug Administration promulgates its regulations and makes its decisions in order to assure that this new policy is in fact fully implemented.

Mr. Justice Frankfurter pointed out thirty years ago that "The history of liberty has largely been the history of observance of procedural safeguards." I am not so naïve as to believe that, simply by improving our procedures, a scientific and lay consensus will be reached on difficult safety issues and our critics will be stilled. Greater public access and representation of divergent viewpoints will, however, inevitably bring with it the beneficial impact that results from any person feeling that he has, in fact, participated in the decision making process.

Second, in addition to guaranteeing more direct and immediate access to the Food and Drug Administration's decision making, we are broadening the base of many of our decisions. Since subjective judgment plays such a large role in safety decisions, we are attempting to make certain that the most informed and respected judgment the country has to offer on these matters is in fact brought to bear on them. During the past three years, the Food and Drug Administration has increasingly relied upon independent technical advisory committees, consisting of scientific experts, to provide advice on major regulatory issues. In the review of over-the-counter drugs and biological products, moreover, we have now gone one step further and included nonvoting consumer and industry members on the technical committees.

It seems clear that, in addition to placing even greater reliance on independent advisory committees in the future, we must begin to include a broader representation of interests on these technical committees, rather than adhering strictly to scientists with specific expertise in the issues immediately before the committee. For as I have already indicated, the difficulties that we encounter in our decisions increasingly involve fundamental philosophical principles and basic questions about the quality of life that trouble our entire society, as well as detailed scientific judgments. Deliberation on these issues properly deserves representation from the entire public.

Third, we are more fully articulating our policy decisions and the reasoning behind them. The public cannot be expected to understand and accept decisions that are nowhere explained. Both the rationale for each decision and any underlying documentation must be laid bare to critical scrutiny.

The Food and Drug Administration has publicly committed itself to this goal with results that have been seen daily in the Federal Register for well over a year. The explanation of our actions, contained in lengthy preambles to new regulations, frequently takes up five to ten times as much space as the regulations themselves. And the procedures for the current review of over-the-counter drugs, biologicals, and in vitro diagnostic products provide for public release of virtually all data provided by the industry -- including volumes of heretofore unpublished scientific information -- upon publication of the proposed regulation.

We have not yet fully solved the problem of making public all of the scientific information that has been accumulating in the Food and Drug Administration since 1906. That is a problem of resources and logistics to do the job, however, and not any desire to retain it as secret. Nor have we yet fully settled the question of what data and information provided to the Food and Drug Administration by industry represents true trade secrets that deserve to be held by us in strict confidence. We are hopeful that both of these problems can successfully be resolved in the near future.

Opening up Food and Drug Administration deliberations in these three ways has, I believe, already substantially improved both our ability to handle difficult safety issues and the public's appreciation of what we are doing. We are, in short, beginning to surmount the obstacles that I have described, and I anticipate enormous further progress in this endeavor in the coming year.

IV

Thus, I am extremely proud of the Food and Drug Administration's recent achievements, and I am very optimistic indeed for its future, in spite of the very difficult obstacles it must overcome to achieve full and fair enforcement of the law. The fact remains that if there were no Food and Drug Administration, one would have to be invented. Some government regulatory agency must be responsible for making the daily decisions as to whether a given food or drug is sufficiently safe to be permitted on the market. The tremendous success of the Food and Drug Administration in carrying out this difficult responsibility is shown by the fact that, in spite of the hundreds of thousands of foods and drugs marketed, the number of known instances of harm that could have been avoided by regulatory action has been extraordinarily small. We intend simply to continue making the most responsible judgments possible on the basis of the best available information and advice, and we welcome the help of everyone who believes, as we do, in the vital importance of this mission to the public welfare.

DISCUSSION

HOGNESS: I see no reason to limit this portion of the discussion to the view-points so well presented by Dr. Lowry and Mr. Hutt. It is also open to the appraisal of some of the subjects that came up earlier. May we have the first question.

IRVING M. LONDON: I am glad that Mr. Hutt addressed the subject of how one effectively engages the public, or public representatives, in the decision making process on public policy issues. I would like to know whether Mr. Turner and Dr. Epstein feel that what is now being done by the Food and Drug Administration, and what is being contemplated, in terms of such involvement of public represen-tatives, consumer representatives and others, is adequate or effective. Are the steps being undertaken by the FDA in line with what its critics were advocating?

HOGNESS: Mr. Turner, would you care to comment?

JAMES S. TURNER: Yes. I started working in the food-drug area and made my first visit to the FDA in March of 1969. I feel very much as if I have been in a fairly long tennis game. We have made some serves, and they have made some returns, and we have made some responses. Let us take just one of the three points that Mr. Hutt made, the information point.

At the time we began to look at the FDA in 1968, it was a totally closed institution, probably more closed than any other in government. I say that advisedly. If you look at their statements under the Freedom of Information Act, they were, at that time, the longest, most detailed statements of exceptions to what would be released by any agency of the government that submitted information on the question.

After we managed to get a few things visible, by having people go against regulations and release information surreptitiously, they turned out to be things that would not cause the crumbling of the nation or even the FDA. As a result, the

132

old policy seemed to be less reasonable.

What happened in the case of Mr. Hutt's taking over and putting out the new Freedom of Information regulation, in my opinion, was a serve to our court. We now have 90 percent of the information that the FDA has in its files available to be read. Please note that I say "available to be read."

An estimate of the bulk of the material done for us by some professional librarians indicated that one to eight million sheets of paper are stuck away in a warehouse somewhere in Virginia. That is probably one of the most incredible caches of information that has ever been available to anyone. I cannot say, in all honesty, that making this material available has solved any problems; but I will say that it offers an opportunity to begin to solve some. So I believe that a step has been taken.

I feel the same way, personally, about the various opportunities that have been developed for consumer and industry liaison people to sit on FDA committees. We are not pleased with the way these committees are operating, and we have made our concerns known. We are concerned about a number of technical details. That the opportunity has been created, however, I view as being valuable.

In other words, I think that we have taken a step, or maybe several steps, toward resolving what was a totally intolerable situation in 1968. I think that we are now beginning to illuminate some of the issues. Before the kinds of things that Mr. Hutt was talking about were begun, there was no dialogue at all. It was just a totally closed and unacceptable situation.

FRANKLIN A. LONG: This is a question to Dr. Lowry. It is very much on the same general subject, however. It seems to me that your principal emphasis as to where the scientist fits in was to highlight his role in technical evaluation of the uses and dangers of drugs via advisory councils or whatever. I would wonder, in a rather general way, whether you would not feel that it is of equal importance that scientists participate pretty actively in the next stage, which is the cost-benefit analysis that leads to policy. I would hope that this would loom rather high on your priority list.

As a quite specific question on that, I wonder what you would have to say about the possibility of independent outside groups -- as for example, departments of pharmacology -- playing a much more significant role in doing independent studies of these things, of applied work directed again to the problem of drug safety, in the newer term, but policy in the large. Is there a role for much more active work outside of government, essentially independent, feeding into policy.

OLIVER H. LOWRY: Very much so. I was about to ask Mr. Hutt exactly the same question. Would it not be possible, at some stage in the testing, that part of the research be delegated to people outside of the drug company concerned? As was pointed out earlier, most of the testing of drugs and the costs of the testing are carried by the drug company interested in that drug. Obviously, it would be impractical to have an equal amount of research done by someone else, but there are certain critical things that might well be checked by impartial outside groups. I would be very much in favor of this.

PETER B. HUTT: Perhaps I could comment on both of those questions. There is no question but that the technical advisory panels, whether they contain the consumer components at this stage (which some of them do) or whether they do not (and unfortunately too many of them at this moment do not), all engage in the benefit-risk analysis. That is part of the safety judgment, and indeed I am not certain that one could extract any particular element of that decision making process and deal only with it in a vacuum.

With regard to use of the academic community for drug testing, perhaps I should explain how drug testing occurs today. There may be others in the audience who wish to discuss it also.

I think that your view is not really the way that it occurs today. For the most part, the pharmaceutical company will give a grant, or directly contract for an independent investigator, usually in the academic community, to undertake the testing. It is not done by employees of the pharmaceutical company. It is almost never done by the Food and Drug Administration -- only very rarely, long after the fact, when we are trying to check up on one particular toxicological aspect of a problem.

In effect, what you describe is being done today. Perhaps John Burns would wish to comment on that aspect of it.

LOWRY: Could I just say that it is one thing to do a research or testing job in which you have nothing at stake and which is paid for by independent funds. It is another thing to accept a grant from a company to test a drug in which it is vitally concerned. When a company recruits someone to do the research and pay the bill, there is always a little worry about unconscious bias. I think that I would be more comfortable if at least some of the research were repeated or extended by someone who had absolutely no stake in it. We all know that there are at least some aspects of drug testing in which bias can easily enter. A company cannot always get its first choice of clinician to test a particular drug. The clinician who finally is persuaded may accept the job because he is in favor of the drug in the first place. This is not good.

W. CLARKE WESCOE: Mr. Chairman, may I comment on that as a long-time former member of the academic community? For the second time today a question has been raised as to whether or not people in pharmaceutical laboratories are as honest as people in the academic world. I would like to state right here that if the people at our research institute were not as honest as were my colleagues at the University of Kansas or at Cornell, they would not be working there today.

Secondly, no one seeks an investigator because he likes a particular product. In fact, I do not think the Food and Drug Administration would accept results from a company if they were submitted from a person known to be untrustworthy. No investigator has any greater stake than his integrity.

What you are saying, Dr. Lowry, is that the academic community cannot be trusted, that they can be bought by someone. As a former member of that community, I do not believe it, and I will not let the statement be made without any protest.

JOHN J. BURNS: Dr. Wescoe expressed pretty much what I would have said. I would just like to comment on one point that was raised earlier and should be stressed -- the dynamic aspect of research in pharmacology-toxicology.

We are living in a changing time, and this produces a paradox. On the one hand you seek new information because it will give better understanding. On the other hand, this new information can create problems. As you obtain more facts, you start to worry about more things. Thus, there is an incentive to seek out information, but there is a discouragement towards this end.

For instance, a few years ago we found that certain drugs stimulate their own metabolism on prolonged administration in chronic toxicity studies in animals. We thought that this was a very interesting pharmacological event, and it stimulated a lot of basic research. We felt that this observation would allow us to interpret toxicity studies better and thus make them more meaningful. However, it also raised questions. Do these toxicity studies mean as much anymore? Should we perhaps do them in a different way? Do the studies really prove the safety of the drug or chemical which is under investigation?

I would like to make a strong plea that we maintain an open mind in the course of research and pharmacology-toxicology. Whether you are working in an academic institution, in a government laboratory, or in a pharmaceutical laboratory, we all share the same dilemma: as we move along we usually find more problems than we can solve.

I was glad to hear Peter Hutt's remarks because I think that there are dynamic aspects to regulation. They cannot be carved in granite. There is a tendency now to look to guidelines as a convenience to help in the design of the "right" type of study, the kind of study that lets us know we have done the necessary work on the drug in question. It would be nice if we could go to the Food and Drug Administration and say, "Please tell us what we should do so that this drug can be approved when the studies are finished four or five years from now." Four or five years from now will be an entirely different world, and the problems will be entirely different. So not only will we have personnel changes in industry but, more importantly, the state of science will have changed at FDA.

One has to look at drug development in a very realistic way. People have criticized work done five or ten years ago which was considered adequate in its time but does not meet present standards. If I am around in ten years, I may think what an inadequate job we did in 1973. We have to look at the changing state of drug research and interpret the regulations within this framework. There must be continued encouragement for innovation in pharmacology-toxicology research. It would be unfortunate if scientists were afraid to explore new areas because this would create more problems and thus raise more questions.

LOWRY: I just want to respond to what my good friend Clarke Wescoe said. I think that if he had told me that some university scientists were not objective, there would have been no disagreement. There are thousands of investigators in the world, and they are certainly not all objective. We have to say, as we go through the literature: "Dan Koshland did it, I know that it is right; X did it, well maybe not." I am not accusing Winthrop or anybody else, but I am sure that Dr. Wescoe would not defend every drug company in the world for objective testing of drugs. I think that it is only wisdom to have some outside checks once in a while.

Let me make this clear. I am not saying that drug companies are any less objective or any more objective than the average scientist. But let us have a double check, particularly in something as important as this. We are not just talking about making a few bucks, we are talking about lives that are at stake.

WESCOE: All I want to comment is that I am not mad; I am upset. No pharmaceutical company worth its salt would allow anybody to do work that would produce dishonest or wrong results. The ultimate liability is so great that the company could not exist. Once more, I wish to support my belief that professors perform responsible investigations.

SAMUEL S. EPSTEIN: I would like to respond to Dr. London's question as to whether I am satisfied with the points Peter Hutt has made. The answer to this is emphatically no. I regard most of the points that Mr. Hutt made as admirable in concept but cosmetic in intent. I would like to be more specific than that. Let me go to the various points without any ranking of priorities.

First of all, the FDA is an interesting organization insofar as the top management is dominated by industrial representation. If one wants to be specific and to examine who makes the decisions in the FDA, and to examine their past records, you will find that a very high percentage of these people come from industry where, as in the defense industry, it is commonplace in this country to have a restricted employment mobility clause to ensure that conflicts of interest be minimized. There is no such attempt to ensure: (a) that people who enter senior decision-making processes in the FDA do not bring with them the constraints and conflicts of interest from industry; and (b) that people who leave the FDA do not go to plum positions in industry which they have regulated hitherto. I would suggest that the first thing that Mr. Hutt should examine is this concept of the revolving door in the FDA.

With regard to freedom of information, there is no question at all in my mind that what Mr. Hutt has said is entirely cosmetic. When we talk about making information available, let us examine what we mean. What is being made available are summaries of toxicological data on safety and efficacy. Now I can take any set of experiments you care to give me and write a summary proving black is white or white is black; and this is precisely what happens. No respectable pathologist or toxicologist places the slightest credence on summaries of toxicological data. For you to suggest that such summaries are meaningful and opening up information to the decision making process is a travesty of information.

My basic position is that at the present moment summaries of information on safety and efficacy of new drugs are just not available and that, therefore, you have not opened up the decision making process to public scrutiny. What you have done is to make available old data, with certain limitations which again we could go into; but as far as new data are concerned, only summaries are available.

One of the other cosmetic attempts and efforts in this direction which the FDA is making are monthly meetings with consumer representatives. These are meetings where issues are raised and aired, and I have attended one or two of them. There have been discussions now, I think, for nearly nine months as to what mechanisms should be developed for scientific and legal representation of consumer and public interest groups in the review of the Generally Recognized As Safe (GRAS) lists by the Federation of American Societies for Experimental Biology (FASEB).

These discussions have an interminable Alice-in-Wonderland flavor. They have been going on for a long time. God knows how much longer they will go on. At every stage in the process the impression is being created that the decision making process is being opened up, but this is illusory. To open up the decision making process, you have to make all data fully and freely accessible to those who have information and who have expertise in the area. Many of the FDA advisory committees are structured and personed by individuals who have very close contacts with industry, who are industrial consultants. The Food Protection Committee of the National Academy of Sciences-National Research Council has been a classic example of the reliance of the FDA in the past on captive groups. There is strong evidence that such linkages still persist.

Let me just make one or two more points. In September of 1972, a memorandum was written by Dr. Johnson of the FDA to Dr. Van Houweling of the FDA, pointing out that FDA policy with regard to feed additives was in gross violation of the law. I can be very specific about this, for it has been the subject of recent Congressional hearings.

The fact is this. The FDA still is currently permitting the use of about seventeen carcinogenic feed additives in food, although no method for measuring residues is available and their continued use is therefore in violation of the law. The same obtains for a wide range of other feed additives, antibiotics, and materials of this kind, for which it is illegal to use these materials in the absence of sensitive methods for measuring residues. As far as an antibiotics are concerned, for instance, there is no method for measuring specifically any particular antibiotic residue.

Now, we found out about this only because the material was leaked. The fact is this. In 1973, for the FDA to control the lives and destinies, the health and

safety and welfare of people, and for us to have to rely on leaked memos and
surreptitious phone calls -- which I constantly get from your staff, Mr. Hutt,
on various issues -- is an intolerable stiuation. It is a situation which does
not allow me to be satisfied with the cosmetic remarks that you have made.

HUTT: It seems to me that there are four questions raised by this, and I
will try to deal with each briefly.

The revolving door issue, I think, is quite a red herring. As a lawyer, I
have never believed in guilt by association or guilt by prior association. I
believe in the integrity of human beings to represent the interests that they are
currently representing. I see no evidence, and I have been on both sides of the
fence, that the high officials in FDA, who may or may not at one time have been
associated with different groups, are derelict in their duty, and I reject very
vehemently any such suggestion.

With reference to the release of data. With regard to food additives, all
safety data on all food additives have been released. Dr. Epstein is incorrect in
his statement.

With regard to drugs. All safety data for antibiotics and all efficacy data
for antibiotics are being released. Dr. Epstein is again incorrect in his information.

With regard to all old drugs and all drugs that have been on the market long
enough to be subject to abbreviated new drug applications, all safety and efficacy
data are being released. Again, he is incorrect there.

Finally, with regard to the new drugs which are largely those that have come
on the market recently, we have not released the safety and efficacy data that have
not otherwise been made available in any form whatever by the company. We have done
that under a statutory prohibition. That statutory prohibition is being litigated

in the courts. We have said that whatever the result of that case, we will abide by it. Either we will continue to make it confidential, or we will start in the future to release it. We will, therefore, be bound by the decision of the court. I have personally testified three times before Congress suggesting that the prohibition against our release of these data be reviewed by Congress to determine whether the law should be changed.

On the monthly consumer meetings. I am fascinated that the suggestion here is that the monthly meeting is the only time that we allow any consumer representative to come into FDA. When I took this job twenty months ago, I told every representative of the consumer interests that they could call me, they could write me at any time, they could get in touch with me any way they wanted, that my door was absolutely open, and that I would do everything that I could to help them. The number of contacts that I have had is probably less than ten in twenty months. There is obviously a lack of resources, and I agree with Mr. Turner on this. This is the fundamental issue -- the lack of lawyers, of scientists, of people who can effectively represent the consumer interests. It is not a lack on the part of FDA to open itself up to their suggestions, recommendations, and petitions.

Now, specifically in the FASEB review of the GRAS list. The problem there -- I think that this in instructive and I would like the views of the Panel for Inquiry on this -- has not been with FDA. It has been FASEB. It is the scientists with whom we have contracted to review the GRAS list, who are not members of FDA, who are protesting the suggestion that they do not represent the public interest and that in some ways there ought to be consumer representation forced upon them. We have asked them to accept it. Unfortunately, that was one of those matters that started well over three years ago when we had not reached our present stage of thinking about consumer input or we would have provided for it right from the beginning.

I would be very much interested in hearing the scientists discuss how the scientific community can be convinced that consumer input is of critical importance.

H. THOMAS AUSTERN: I have a double-barreled question to address to Dr. Lowry and Mr. Hutt. But I want to preface it with a very brief comment on Dr. Epstein's observations on cosmetic changes. I am qualified to comment, I suggest, on the basis of geriatrics, having been in the field since 1931. As one who lives with these matters daily, I regard these changes not as cosmetic but as systemic.

Now my question relates, if we can get back to the subject, to the participation of consumer and industry representatives at an early stage in the decision making process. I would like to approach that without these ad hominem and denigrating observations on the academic community, the industrial community, or the regulators.

TURNER: How about the consumers?

AUSTERN: I will be with you in a moment.

It was Dr. Lowry who, I think, advanced the suggestion that there should be advisory panels. I want to make it clear, sir, that for twenty-five years, publicly and on the Hill, I have objected to them because they did work in closets. I believe that they were subjected to lobbying. There was no record of their deliberations or of the compromises that might have been achieved. Nevertheless, where do you stand on having consumer panels at these preliminary stages? That is for Dr. Lowry.

On the other side of the coin, I would like to ask Mr. Hutt whether, in his view, the FDA can ever abdicate its responsibility because of the recommendations of an advisory panel? As a footnote, if you answer that, I hope that Mr. Turner will turn to Mr. Hutt's third improvement and tell me what he thinks of preambles. My views on that are on record, but the preambles were not mentioned either by Mr. Turner or by Dr. Epstein.

LOWRY: In regard to the representatives from the general public, I think that this would be great. I think that if the public is sufficiently interested to sit through all of the scientific discussions, it would be marvelous. I think this would be welcome not only for some of the advisory committees of the FDA, but also for the advisory committees of NIH.

I might say that I think that I rate almost as high geriatrically as you, Mr. Austern. I think that I was almost on the first NIH study section. I would say, in contrast to your point of view, that although I am pretty sensitive to the possibility of log rolling, I have never, in all these years, seen any evidence of it in these "secret" panel or study section sessions. Sometimes there are certain things that are kept secret because we may have said bad things about some investigators who did not meet the criteria and the objectivity which we have just been discussing. Otherwise, there is nothing secret about any of these meetings, and there are representatives present from across the board, from private institutions, public institutions, and the like.

I feel very strongly that this NIH study section organization is one of the most effective review systems ever set up. I would like to see it extended to the FDA.

HUTT: We have, of course, begun to extend it and are in the process of extending it still further.

However, let me give a specific answer to Mr. Austern's question: The Commissioner of Food and Drugs, under the law, is obligated to make the decision, and he will make the decision. The use of advisory committees is, as I mentioned earlier, to broaden the base of input into that decision, to make certain that the most informed judgment available in the country is brought to bear on it. I can give one very brief example.

We now have data that apparently -- and not being a scientist I must repeat what others have told me -- showed that if you feed FD&C Red No. 2 to test animals in their ordinary diet, there is no particular toxicological problem. But if you feed it by gavage, there is indeed a toxicological problem. The issue on what we do on FD&C Red No. 2 then resolves down to whether gavage is relevant to human consumption. I am unaware whether there happens to be a jury of scientists in the country who are the world's experts on gavage --

HOGNESS: Since you are a medical expert, Mr. Hutt, will you define for the audience what you mean by gavage?

HUTT: As I understand it, that is direct feeding, by tube, into the stomach. If I am wrong, please correct me.

This is not an issue in which one looks to the medical textbook and achieves an instant answer. We went to the National Academy of Sciences. An ad hoc committee concluded that it was not particularly relevant, although not wholly irrelevant. We then consulted both with our own scientists and with one or two selected outside experts of a different kind. They said that it was probably more relevant than irrelevant.

We are now, tomorrow morning, convening another group of ad hoc consultants who, we hope, can shed some further light on this very difficult issue.

Now the Commissioner of Food and Drugs ultimately must decide that. But obviously on a very subtle, very difficult, very judgmental issue such as this, we need the best judgment that we can get. If anyone has an opinion, incidentally, I would be glad to take it back.

TURNER: I guess I am to respond to your question, Mr. Austern, as to what is my opinion of the preambles. Let me clarify for the audience what the issue here is, as I understand it, although I am not sure that any of us understands it clearly. When the FDA issues a regulation, there is a section of it which essentially becomes

146

the law. One of the innovations, the one that was third on Mr. Hutt's list, was a series of paragraphs that precede a piece of law which purport to tell us why that piece of law is being adopted. Mr. Austern questions the value of this material. You cannot use it in court, he would argue, I think.

AUSTERN: We would.

TURNER: You would. I am not sure. It is unclear as to what category it is or what authority it has. As I understand your position -- you might want to clarify it -- you want the regulation to be in the regulations.

AUSTERN: I have not said a word. You were invited to comment on three improvements suggested by Mr. Hutt. I noted the fact that you devoted a good bit of attention to two of them; but the third one, which in your profession has excited great interest, you did not comment on. I am inviting comment. I do not want to debate with you.

TURNER: I was trying to clarify what the issue is. You see an issue there. I see it as being a way to inform people, and it does not bother me. What does bother me, however, is that on a number of occasions, in my opinion, what is said in the regulation is not necessarily reflective of what is said in the preamble. That does bother me, and I have one in my hand that concerns me.

This is one on vaccines, which was just released. It talks about the fact that unavoidable bacteriophages have been found in vaccines just recently. What concerns me is that there is a long discussion to the effect that this is not a safety problem; but then the regulation says, "Product shall be free from extraneous material, except for unavoidable bacteriophages." There is no indication of what will happen if it turns out that a bacteriophage is in fact unsafe, so that we will be stuck with the regulation which, in fact, makes it legal to have something in a vaccine which is not safe, even though the preamble is premised on the assumption that there is inherent safety here. From my point of view, there may very well be some scientific questions. It concerns me that if we have to go into court to fight this kind of an issue, we will be delaying what I think would be a reasonable decision that could be made quite rapidly if it were not for this regulation. I happen to think that this is in violation of the law, and I would challenge it on those grounds. We are going to make a submission, by the way.

AUSTERN: Since you are now informed, do you believe having those preambles is an improvement?

TURNER: Yes. But that brings me to the point of commenting on Dr. Epstein's position. You see, whether or not he is right that these improvements are intended to be cosmetic, for all practical purposes at the present moment, they are cosmetic changes, partially because the resource imbalance exists. In addition to that, there are some very strong problems of how we proceed from here on out.

I have sat now on the first of the vaccine committees. I am concerned about the tendency that goes on there -- one that I am afraid has been going on when I was not sitting there, but bothers me even more that it is going on when I sit there. Here, for example, is a man who says: "I believe that this vaccine should not be on the market. I believe that it should come off the market. However, there are six million doses of it in use, which means somebody wants it. Therefore, I must bend over backwards to be careful that I do not take an action against it because of my own personal bias." Now, I say that that is a difficult problem, and I think that it is very much the problem that you were talking about. I am very pleased that it is something that we can talk about publicly.

HUTT: Are you not also pleased that you are there to hear it and to participate in the process? If that is true, is not the process working?

TURNER: I am saying that I am glad that we are there for that kind of a discussion, but I am trying to suggest that the kinds of discussions which seem perfectly acceptable to you, i.e., saying that this man is not objective, are not really unbiased discussions. They are discussions which are of extreme importance. Some of the most significant supporters of consumer science have been, on various occasions, labeled as unacceptable for scientific reasons in a way that I find not too pleasant. It smacks of an effort to keep people out who are saying things that are not widely accepted, rather than keeping them out on the basis of other infor- mation, on basis of qualification. I think that is a very important issue on which there should be public conversation and involvement. To that extent, I think that they are good, but I do not think they are in fact as yet doing much more than if they were cosmetic.   I believe that they probably have a potential to do more if the resource imbalance is corrected.

EPSTEIN: I would like to respond to Mr. Hutt, who succeeded in misquoting me on four occasions, which is particularly interesting as he only made five points.

First of all, as far as the availability or access to information, I said that data on safety and efficacy for new drugs are available only in summary form. That is what I said. I made no reference to food additives in regard to access of data. However, as he raised the question of food additives, let me point out the fact that I have repeatedly asked the FDA for information on safety and efficacy data on some food additives. Both Mr. Turner and I have in our possession a letter from Dr. Wodicka of the FDA in which he states categorically, clearly, and unequivo- cally that only summaries of toxicological data are available. The rest of the data are considered confidential. If Mr. Hutt would like to assure this audience now that the policy has changed with relation to petitions on food additives, I would be delighted to hear this.

As far as FASEB is concerned, the playing of games between FDA and FASEB has gone on for some time. I would suggest that if the FDA is really serious about getting consumer representation on FASEB review committees of the GRAS list, they indicate that they propose to cancel the contract with FASEB unless these recommendations for consumer representation are developed.

With a final comment on FD&C Red No. 2, Mr. Hutt has made a reference to the appointment of an FDA ad hoc committee on gavage. The appointment of this particular committee illustrates our general sense of unease about some aspects of FDA procedures. The chairman of this committee is an individual with long historic associations with industry as an industrial consultant and in other capacities. He repeatedly has taken the position that gavage is unnatural -- something like a deep throat type of phenomenon -- and that gavage being unnatural, the toxicological data developed by it are somehow challengable. This is extraordinarily interesting.

Gavage is the standard method for the administration of carcinogens. Pharmaceutical industries and the food industry use it routinely. If data are negative with gavage tests, I have never heard of industry having raised an objection to the use of such a technique. It is only with positive data, in the one instance of the FD&C Red No. 2 where it is positive by gavage and negative by feeding, that the questions have been raised.

Let me point out that gavage is very closely related to drinking. In other words, if a child takes a bottle of soda pop containing Red No. 2, the effects of this will be very similar to gavage. Of course, when you mix material in the dye, the greater absorption is spread out and delayed for long periods of time.

It is, as I said before, the standard test method for carcinogenicity and toxicity testing. If, indeed, the FDA wishes to have expert advice, I would suggest that they would do better to select as a chairman for this committee a person who already has taken public stands, who is constrained by his own personal interests.

Another member of this committee was the chairman of the so-called FDA Advisory Committee on 2,4,5,-T, which came out with the statement that low levels of environmental teratogens are not particular harmful. I would suggest that this is illustrative of our concerns in the FDA procedures in such matters.

JOSEPH COOPER: Mr. Chairman, I wonder if we are not concerning ourselves unduly with what we might call venality dynamics. We do not trust anyone who has had real world experience in working with drugs because to get that you must have had a relationship with the sponsoring firms. If you have done that, then you are disqualified. You are a crook, or potentially so. In any event, like Caesar's wife, you do not have the appearance of being pure or chaste or whatever. You are forever proscribed. How many years you must go through proscription is something that we must determine. We should have an ad hoc committee on that, with a balanced participation.

It is a real problem because I think that what we are doing is proscribing creative dynamics. We are using up the creative energies of people who ought to devote themselves to innovation and to testing out the safety and efficacy of innovation. I have a little minor claim to geriatrics, having observed the FDA for about a dozen years. If you look toward the summit, it is a long, long road up to that summit. But if you look back at how far the FDA has climbed, I think that it deserves a great deal of commendation. And I say this knowing that I probably could make as long a list of things that I can criticize about the FDA as anybody in this room.

The third kind of dynamics that concerns me is the great preoccupation with prudence dynamics, safety to the ultimate. If you do not have a good reason to prove that something is unsafe, it is prudent not to take the risk. At a meeting at the Food and Drug Law Institute, I made a suggestion to somebody from one of the big companies on the Delaney amendment. Take some milk of human breast and take all the breakdown products of the milk and then feed them torrentially by gavage, or any

other route, to rats. As Dr. Wescoe said, they probably would die of something else before carcinogenesis occurs. I am sure that something in there would be ruled out.
PHILIP HANDLER: Lactose.

COOPER: Yes. Leave the DDT out of this one just as a matter of courtesy. We have had I do not know how many billions of participants in clinical experimentation at their mother's breast, and we ought to be able to get some real world epidemiology out of that. Someone has said that we need to bypass the dog and get into man. Anyway, the point is taken that we are really dealing with medication in man -- medication of a variety of types. Some of them offer us more of a problem, like social products, contraceptives, than those that are therapeutic.

There was a comment from the Panel for Inquiry about a stepped approach, and perhaps we ought to spend more time on such an approach so that under monitored investigation we could move progressively into the real world to see what actually happens. This could be done much more economically than having all kinds of mass tests of sophistication in the interest of prudence dynamics. Moreover, the products would be a real world dimension on safety and more innovation. If you study the history of innovation, it comes out of clinical experience, where a side reaction -- something that we want to throw out -- is picked up and used constructively. Or some other effect that was unanticipated by the investigator is picked up and used therapeutically. There are so many examples of it.

On the other hand, we can pick up so many of the prudence examples. Penicillin would not be here if it were not tested in the guinea pig. We just would not have it. The whole history of therapeutics would have been changed.

I would like to make one final comment. We are really preoccupied with the organization of advisory committees. We have come a long, long way, and I think that we are headed in the right direction. I would be more worried, perhaps, about advisory committees being co-opted by the staff of the FDA than I would be about the FDA being co-opted by the advisory committees. Once the committees get together and are sufficiently neutralized among themselves in their dialogue, the staff can readily take over.

There are some risks, and they ought to be examined. But what we have is so much superior to what we have had in the past that we just should, in good humor, say how do we improve this and then take the next leap forward.

Thank you, for all this time.

HOGNESS: I was just admiring your lung capacity. I was trying to interrupt you when you took a breath, and you never did take one.

CHARLES SNODGRASS: I work for the House of Representatives, and I first would comment that I think that a deficiency here today, with all due respect, is that there is no one to represent the legislative point of view. Many of the things that you are talking about today ultimately will have to go into that arena.

Next, I would like to ask any of the participants what the Congress should do to change its decision making processes so as to do a better job? The reason I ask this question is that until Mr. Hutt spoke today, I think that if you had taken a poll of the 435 members of the House, a majority of them would have told you that cyclamates were banned because of the Delaney clause. Now, if this is not true, there is something wrong with the information process, and we need to change it. I would like to know how do we change it?

HUTT: I could respond very briefly to that. The changes necessary in the law -- to go either to the type of step process that Dr. Morrison mentioned, the type of flexibility that Dr. Lederberg is interested in, the type of thing in which I am interested in getting more data out to the public -- are somewhat trivial. They do not get to the heart of the issue of what I call the full and fair enforcement of the law. Most of these changes, except for getting the data out, could be instituted tomorrow if we had the insight to know the best way of doing them.

So, fundamental issues here are ones of greater scientific understanding and information, greater policy judgment. They are not basically legislative issues.

AUSTERN: Mr. Chairman, I have one suggestion for the gentleman who inquired about what Congress might do to be helpful. One thing that I think impedes the regulatory process, and has for many decades, is the practice on the Hill of hauling in regulatory officials, be it from the Bureau of Medicine or from the Bureau of Foods, to be interrogated by a committee or its staff. There they are put in the position, despite their basis of reasonable good faith and dedicated judgment, of being made to look either venal or stupid. Congress's right to investigate is paramount, but if you are going to look in and do a post hoc, postmortem judgment on what the regulators have decided, you ought to do it in camera, as it is done by the Atomic Energy Commission.

HOGNESS: I take it, however, that the remark there was made primarily toward suggesting congressional participation in forums such as these in the future.

JOSHUA LEDERBERG: I would like to discuss a few somewhat general issues. I think that Mr. Snodgrass ought to meet with Mr. Daddario in respect to some possible answers to your question, a resource that might be of some use in that regard. I think that there are some promising developments in that direction that Mr. Daddario was so instrumental in arousing attention in and ultimate approval for.

A number of things have come up that I think tend to show differences in point of view. I will start with the notion of conflict of interest. A lot has been said about venality or mendacity. I have even greater faith in the human capacity for self-delusion, which in itself is capable of generating so much mischief.

Occasional examples of venality and corruption can very well be taken care of by the laws. But just a sense of prudence about the way in which people think in ambiguous situations would suggest that if you want to be sure you have thoroughly ventilated a situation, you want to find people who are capable of holding completely outrageous and irrational positions, who will be looking for trouble against all contrary evidence, and who will have no reason to be beholden in any way to people who might regard that as bad news. This is not because of explicit lack of integrity, but just the way all of us work in marginal situations. Should we put out a further balance of effort when we have had a very long day and have innumerable choices to make in pursuing a flicker of a possible source of trouble? Or should we just go ahead, and finish up the report, and do the job that was expected? This is a perfectly legitimate alternative kind of response. I think that all of us have had these kinds of experiences and know to what I am referring. It does not repute any lack of integrity or dishonesty among academic scientists any more than it does among industrialists.

Mr. Hutt referred to the dilemma about the interpretation of gavage, and it is very interesting to see how different people react to that circumstance. He saw it as a problem in regulation, of how do you end up making a decision. Is gavage relevant or not relevant to the question of the toxicity of the drug? Dr. Epstein wants to know who is paying whom in trying to reach that kind of a conclusion.

The reaction I had to it is that this may be a fantastic research opportunity, and nothing was mentioned about the implications. The different routes of administration, if I understand what was said, are giving very clear cut differences in a carcinogenic response without there being an obvious rationale, a very clear cut rationale, for that case. It may well be a simple matter of the timing of the introduction into the circulation. But one can build models to describe possible consequences of different routes of administration, see if they fit, and then not only will have solved the problem about the relevance of gavage in certain sets of circumstances, but one will have gotten a deeper understanding of the basic mechanisms. It is the urgent search for that kind of spillover and that kind of generalization from safety research that I think has to be injected into further development.

HUTT: I would just like to make one comment directly on point there. The issue that we must face, as I have pointed out in my remarks, is what do we do tomorrow, not what do we do two years from now when we get the results of your research.

LEDERBERG: But then that research never gets done. The issue will be put on the shelf. And you will be facing that same problem, and you will be investing the same effort over and over again in ad hoc situations. I think that you must find a way in which you can get other resources to deal with it at that level.

Mr. Hutt also made some remarks that were consistent with a number of other statements of the kind that many scientists make, namely, that there is an absolute wall between the rigorous scientific demonstration and that rather loose and fuzzy area called values. That is an overreaction to a trend that one might have heard fifteen, twenty, thirty years ago, that science was the answer not only to problems about the facts of nature, but also the issues of religion and ethics. Many of us have swung sharply off in the other direction, and I think too far.

Philip Handler, inadvertently, made a somewhat similar kind of remark, although it is inconsistent with his general outlook. There is a very profound connection between knowledge and ethics. If you know the consequences of your microscopic acts, you can make wise choices, based on some experience, rather than continue to flounder around. There are solutions to a problem that do not just have to be put into a closet called value judgment, after which you walk away from them and simply bear the consequences.

Finally, I think that there is a very deep issue that no one really has mentioned: Why do we need a regulatory agency at all? What are the implications for the reliability of our physicians across the country if they have to be policed in this fashion, in this great detail, and there must be a centralized decision on whether a drug is allowed or is not allowed to be used for various circumstances? I am astonished that the medical profession has not reacted very much more strongly not only in aggrievance against this kind of policing, but in somewhat more constructive ways about trying to take a more positive role in managing its own affairs. What does it mean with respect to every other aspect of health service? We confide our lives to a doctor's judgment. Many areas of his actions are not policed, only his decisions as to which kinds of drugs might be available. (Many of the compounds that are passed by FDA can kill you, too, if they are inappropriately used.) Plainly, there has been a judgment that physicians generally -- there must be numerous exceptions, and my own doctor, needless to say, is one of them -- are incompetent to make these decisions for themselves.

This is a point for which there is, unfortunately, some documentation, although by and large it is more in the direction of the rather careless use of unnecessary drugs than it is in the aggressive use of very toxic ones. But we have seen too many examples of the latter as well. Before we can make too many voices in the wilderness about this, however, it seems to me that we need much more actual information on doctors' prescribing behavior, on what are the sources of their information, on the judgments that they make. How bad is it? How bad would it really be if they were given more latitude, and if the police (the FDA) were given less, in terms of decisions as to what was lawful and what was not lawful to be used in that practice?

Inevitably, with the police, with the best intentions, with the deepest of wisdom, and with all of the very constructive and positive changes, there has to be a bureaucracy. There has to be a book of rules. There have to be precedents. You end up with circumstances where not always the most competent people are in charge of the most important decisions that affect the lives of many of us. I think that there are very sound reasons to wish that we could have a much more pluralistic system of judgment in areas of this kind, or find some point at which there will be a stop with respect to the police role in the registration of a whole variety of consumer products. We need much more actual information before we can begin to decide on these kinds of policies.

HOGNESS: Thank you, Dr. Lederberg. Dr. Koshland wants to make a remark. I will then call for comments from the audience.

DANIEL E. KOSHLAND, JR.: We regret not having someone from Congress on the program. We are quite aware of the strong interplay in these matters among the various branches of government. However, we have tried to give you the broadest spectrum of viewpoints possible within the limited time.

A subject about which I feel strongly was mentioned in part by Dr. Lederberg and touched on by other speakers. It relates to the FDA's problems and Congress's decision making. We have learned in this discussion that these issues are much more complex than they appear in the newspapers. I hope that one achievement of this Forum will be to convey to Congress and other lay groups that when the FDA is asked to make an early decision, it sometimes must be made on very imperfect data.

For example, Dr. Lederberg's mention of the extrapolation from a thousand rats to 2×10^8 humans is really not an extrapolation that anybody knows or understands today. Whether the extrapolation is linear, concave downward, or concave upward is vital, but we do not know the answer. That does not mean that I advocate scrapping the Delaney amendment. But when somebody oversimplifies and says that they really know cyclamate is bad, they should be corrected. There is a probability that cyclamate is harmful. That is all we can say. If we are going to cut the cost of drug research and make more rational decisions on tight time scales, we will have to do more basic research and obtain a fundamental understanding. Only then will we be able to extrapolate from lower forms of life to higher forms of life.

Another question was raised by Mr. Hutt in wondering why the resistance of FASEB to constituting the GRAS list review panels. It is my understanding that FASEB thought, in part, that it was asked to make a technical decision. To put lay members on a committee to make a technical decision is resisted by some scientists. They say, "All right. If the public wants to make a terrible mistake after we give them the data, that is their responsibility. At least, we are going to tell them what that risk is."

In fact, as we all know, some of these decisions are not that easily separated between science and public values. I think that scientists need education on the one side, and some of us are working toward this. But the public also has to recognize that there are very complicated technical issues involved, and it is not easy to divide it up between the bad guys and the good guys.

In closing, I would like to suggest that Mr. Daddario make a brief comment on the complexities of the congressional and scientific interface.

HOGNESS: I will give him a chance to think about that for a moment while I call on two other people.

MARSHA N. COHEN: I am from Consumers Union. I would like to point out that consumers did not ask for lay representation on the FASEB review panels for the GRAS list. All the names we suggested were those of qualified scientists. So it was not a question of laymen participating in a scientific group. I also would like to hear Mr. Hutt's comments on what, if anything, the FDA has done to pressure FASEB. I assume the FDA has pressure at its command, but that is not my major point.

HUTT: I will confirm that we are exerting appropriate pressure.

COHEN: I was reminded by Dr. Cooper's remark a few people ago that there is one issue that has not really been discussed. He mentioned the milk of human breast. I think this is a rather ridiculous example, with all respect to him, because we all concede the benefits of that product. However, we have forgotten that there is a benefit side of the equation supposedly in regard to such products as Red No. 2. Nobody discussed what these benefits, if any, are. I would like to hear people discuss how they see the benefit side of the equation for colors, fragrances, flavors, and such other incidental items.

RICHARD L. HALL: You have presented me with an opportunity I can no longer avoid. I think that it is easy and a temptation to attempt to construct a hierachy of values with certain types of technical effects for food additives, such as preservatives and nutrients, at one high end and then progressing down to presumably less useful, or socially useful, types of activity. In fact, I think, it is a faulted, flawed analysis that falls under the weight of critical examination. It does so because, as Dr. Lederberg said earlier, there is, in fact, an infinite number of exchanges that can be made here. We could do without sulfur dioxide, for example, but bottles of wine would be of less reliable quality and more expensive. We could do without all preservatives, but we would give up many food items. We would give up a considerable amount of variety. We would suffer increased costs and lowered acceptability.

Now, we could do this with, in fact, every category of food additives, including colors. We do not need color, supposedly, except of course in the sense that color, flavor, texture, mouth feel, and temperature are in fact the bases on which we make most of our food choices, even though they may seem to be less important and less rational than nutrition and safety. In fact, consumer choices often frustrate the

the best efforts of regulators and industry alike.

Until we recognize the physiological importance of these so-called subjective factors, and their contribution to food quality and nutrition, we will forever fall into this trap of assuming that some things are more important than others. We all find it very easy to be cavalier about the preferences of others and remain very resentful of any effort to change our own.

EMILIO DADDARIO: Mr. Chairman, I have listened with interest and pleasure to this discussion because what we have is a Forum where divergent points of view are being brought to bear in a very forceful fashion. It would be impossible in the time remaining for me to develop a thesis about the interface between the scientific community and the Congress. However, I would add this. It does become important that the scientific community, as a part of the entire community, and as every other part of the social structure, must develop a way to fit into the process of government so that discussion can take place before the fact rather than after the fact. This is the only way divergent points of view can be brought to bear during the decision making process rather than afterwards. This can be done and is being done, and it is being improved in the Congress and has been over the course of the last decade or so by a closer working relationship between the Congress and the scientific community.

For example, a dozen years ago the Congress formed a contract with the National Academy of Sciences which was the first formal contract the Congress had ever had with the Academy in its over one hundred years of existence. At that time the Academy had been oriented toward the Executive Branch, and it had difficulty in dealing with the Congress. I think that this relationship has improved and includes improved scientific capabilities of congressional staffs and in the Library of Congress, as well as improved advisory relationships with the scientific and technical community. In the process of doing this, people had the opportunity not only for discussions, but to develop a relationship which is one of greater confidence and greater ease than in the past.

It is always necessary to bring people together as early as possible. You can make decisions on your own, but eventually the facts have to be faced, and they are usually faced later rather than earlier with great emotion. Decisions then become emotionally stimulated rather than rational. I do believe that people on the whole are honest and have great integrity. They want to state their own position; but if they have an opportunity to rub their ideas against others, they will recognize where their weaknesses are and where their strengths are, as will people on the other side. Problems can be rationalized and brought together much easier by bringing forces of conflict together rather than by waiting for them to come in conflict. This has been pointed out here today in regard to situations where doors have been closed and, in the long run, would be better opened and would cause less conflict than at present. It is a matter of the need for more openness and more dependency on each other than has been the case in the past.

HOGNESS: I thank all of you in the audience for your comments. I am sorry that we cannot hear from more of you. I will now turn to the speakers to ask if they have any concluding remarks.

TURNER: I have a couple of points to make.

First of all, I think that the last thing that Dr. Lederberg said is extremely important: what is really necessary before we can begin to make some of the more abstract judgments applicable to our situation is to learn what that situation is. It means that we need to do a great deal more looking at facts. This means not only the scientific facts, but some of the real facts which we know to exist or which at least appear to exist.

We have talked about conflict of interest, for example. I personally am concerned by the evidence collected by the Health Research Group that it is not an uncommon practice in clinical testing to pay the clinical tester in stocks of the company which is having the drug tested. I find this conflict of interest difficult to sort out, and I think that it is something that should be looked at, examined, and perhaps banned.

I was interested in Dr. Lederberg's comments on the Peltzman paper. If you will recall -- and I am sorry that his slide is not here because I wanted to refer to some of the points -- it showed that in 1959 there was a precipitous drop in single chemical new entities that have arrived on the market. This line dropped until 1963, when there was a fluctuating line that went out to 1968. Somebody had written "Kefauver" at the point of the drop on the graph. It has become a common notion, in the minds of many people, that somehow Kefauver did something at that point that caused these things to happen. It is very similar to the old system of killing the messenger who brought the bad news. What Kefauver did was to point out that in the FDA there was a tremendous conflict between the interests of one of its primary regulators. He had interests in an industrial situation, a regulatory situation, and he was making money to the tune of $225,000 in this very fortuitous situation.

I suggest that it might well be that the precipitous drop resulted from a lack of confidence generated by the news that Kefauver brought and that, in fact, the creation of the new laws in 1963 stopped that drop and restored some confidence. If you will look from 1963 on, the average for new introductions varied up and down, but the average has been constant.

Finally, I just must reiterate the Salk incident as I presented it to try to illustrate what I think is a specific problem. I think that placing 260 injuries and 10 deaths against perhaps 100,000 cases of polio is the way we tend to look at that incident in abstract. But if we look at the facts of how it developed, it was a mere thirty days from the time the problems were discovered until they were completely corrected and the vaccine was back on the market. It seems to me that that thirty days could have been energized somewhere prior to the mass immunization campaign. Specifically, since there was some suggestion of a problem on a practical experimental basis as well as a theoretical basis in the laboratories of the regulatory agency, it seems to me that it was the responsibility to take the thirty days to do what what was necessary in the six months that transpired between the discovery of a problem and the final incident.

All I am suggesting is that we need to look very closely at that kind of a situation to see what it is, what pressures, what drives, what motivations caused these decisions not to be made.

Finally, just to sum it up, we have been told how the turtle only advances when he sticks his neck out. I would like to point out that turtles make their progress very slowly and deliberately. I think that is the way we must make ours in these areas.

HOGNESS: Thank you. Dr. Wescoe, do you have any comments?

WESCOE: I believe in a beatitude that is very little known: "Blessed is he who has nothing to say and steadfastly resists the opportunity to say it."

HOGNESS: Bless you. Dr. Lowry?

LOWRY: Nothing further --

HUTT: I have nothing to add.

HOGNESS: I will now call on the five members of the Panel for Inquiry for any concluding remarks they wish to make. Dr. London?

IRVING M. LONDON: There has been mention of the need for much new knowledge, and I would like to underline that. Dr. Lederberg mentioned briefly the role of genetics. I think that the field of pharmacal genetics needs a great deal of further development with regard to the possible toxicity of various agents.

One area for basic research which certainly could stand much greater support is that of seeking biological systems in which subtle preclinical changes could be demonstrated. I think that the problem of clinical testing is a very difficult and very important one. I might point out that the clinical research centers sponsored by the NIH provided a mechanism for such clinical testing under controlled conditions. Cutbacks in support of these centers do not make such clinical testing easier. There are difficult legal and ethical problems in regard to testing drugs in patients. There certainly are difficult problems when such testing is done with prisoners. These issues must be addressed more directly than they have been.

Now I think that when we talk about engagement of the public in public policy determination, we really are talking about the development of an informed public and of representatives who are informed. With regard to health hazards and the role of chemical agents in our environment, this public education lags very far behind the need for it.

Too little, I think, has been said about the physician's role in the prescription of drugs and in the use of them. Allusion was made to that a moment ago. I think that it is incumbent on those of us in medicine to pay far more attention to the education of practicing physicians both in medical school and in the immediate postdoctoral period. The practicing physician, to too great an extent, is getting his information from sources that are not wholly impartial or objective. Indeed, much of the information that the practicing physician gets is from organizations that are trying to sell products and, obviously, are trying to present their products in the best possible light. This is not always the most accurate setting for such education of a physician.

I would say that if we are indeed to have appropriate public engagement in public policy determination, and if we are to have the kind of data base on which intelligent decision making can be made, we need much more education of the public and the providers of health service. We need much more research on the basis of which information can be provided.

HOGNESS: Thank you. Dr. McCarty?

MACLYN McCARTY: I would like to reemphasize the matter of the biological complexity of testing drugs both for efficacy and for safety. I think that this matter has been alluded to by several speakers. Most of the important elements that are involved in this complexity have been touched upon at one time or another during the day, including such things as the serious problem of extrapolating from animal experiments to man, the problems of variation in drug metabolism in different species, and the difficulties of trying to set up models for testing in a reliable way for any of these various types of toxicity that result in things like carcinogenicity, teratogenicity, or mutagenicity.

It is a problem, in effect, that is very much like the problem of biological research in general, one which is multifactorial with numerous variables which are very difficult to control. It is made much worse in this situation by the absolute necessity of ultimately going to man for the final determination of either efficacy or safety. Therefore, I think that we are probably asking of it a degree of assurance and certainty which is going to be very difficult to achieve and can only be approached, in the long run, by redoubling the kinds of efforts that have been made.

HOGNESS: Thank you. Dr. Adams?

ROBERT McC. ADAMS: In the detailed, multihued fabric of our discussion there have been at least a few connecting strands. One that emerged implicitly at many points, and that was made explicit by Dr. Lowry, is that the responses of human organisms to drugs and food additives are highly complex, variable, and poorly understood. From the viewpoint of the scientist, this led him to place appropriate stress on the importance of sustained federal support for basic research -- without which further advances will be tragically slower and more dangerous. The point is in no sense limited to the theme of this Forum, of course, but it deserves renewed emphasis as we draw together the threads of our exploration of issues of great practical concern within the setting of the National Academy of Sciences.

From the somewhat different viewpoint of the regulatory agency, Mr. Hutt advanced in a different direction from the same underlying generalization. Regulation must go forward, he reminded us, "in the midst of unresolvable scientific disagreement" on the meaning of test results and in the absence of public or scientific consensus on acceptable levels of risk. The problems of the Food and Drug Administration are compounded, he also noted, by the fact that an absolute absence of risk can never be demonstrated. The calculus of cost clearly must include the consequences of delays in the introduction of beneficial new drugs as well as the direct expense of massive testing programs. But in any case there remains "an inescapable but undeterminable risk" associated with the marketing of any new product.

Faced with these conditions, the FDA must act, as Mr. Hutt has observed within "a very broad and general mandate rather than upon narrow and specific rules." As James Q. Wilson has noted in a rather skeptical overview of the performance of regulatory agencies generally ("The Dead Hand of Regulation," The Public

Interest, Fall 1971), this avoidance of rules is a strikingly common feature. Uncertainty amplifies the power of agencies to control corporate behavior, he explains, while at the same time -- to the annoyance of the consumerists -- agencies tend to consider that modifications of rules unnecessarily restrain the particularistic judgments required in individual cases. In any case, the FDA's objective is to improve and make more explicit the balance of risks and benefits; but the balance is thus broadly conceived and seldom can be directly translated into testing protocols or standards of purity. And decisions must be made within finite, if probably somewhat elastic, time and budgetary constraints, all the while subject to considerable pressures from a variety of interest groups.

In spite of their disagreement with Mr. Hutt on other issues, the consumer interests for which Mr. Turner is a spokesman seemingly are sensitive to the FDA's difficult predicament. I doubt that Mr. Hutt would disagree with Mr. Turner's characterization of both risks and benefits as highly aggregative categories, all of whose quite disparate constituents must be traced out individually and kept in account. Nor is a simple producer-consumer dichotomy adequate, as the important economic benefits of DES, and perhaps DDT, for broad sectors of consumers suggest. Under the circumstances, I'm inclined to conclude that Mr. Turner is right in stressing the limitations on the role of scientists in decision making within at least the drug and food additive area. Scientific advice, in the sense of laboratory experimentation, peer review panels and the like, is an indispensable constituent in the policy decisions that the FDA somehow must make. But by itself scientific advice is not sufficient as a basis for most of those decisions.

My fundamental concern for the social process of decision making leads me now to raise a question for Mr. Hutt that I decided against posing soon after he spoke. I felt that there was inherent contradiction between his description of himself as a strong advocate of the adversary process at one point and then, in another context, speaking rather pejoratively of trial by combat versus reasoned decision making.

The reason that I decided not to do so was that it struck me that we were groping here with a kind of social invention, if I can call it that. In fact, this Forum is an attempt to define wider uses for, shall we call it, the adversary process, to define a set of procedural safeguards that make it possible for people of divergent points of view to come together and to present sharply opposed points of view. It is all very well to say that this is done in the courts; but there are, of course, hundreds of years in the development of procedural safeguards there. And I guess there is, above all else, a judge who can act as the all powerful umpire.

Here, we are dealing with a different set of circumstances. Of course in the Forum itself we decoupled it from the surrounding immediate problems and therefore it becomes possible. As I felt through to Mr. Hutt's problem, I wondered how far can this simply be picked up and applied in a regulatory agency? At what point does the broadening out of the range of opinions that are being offered simply increase the random noise level and decrease the possibilities of dealing with the fundamental issues on which judgment must turn? I do not mean to suggest that I have an answer to that, but it does seem to me that it requires on the part of government officials a very great deal of care and caution as they move in this direction.

In some respects the general view that I have gotten of Mr. Turner's argument, for example, is that he regards the Delaney amendment as a convenient shield, so to speak, behind which it should be possible for the consumer forces to marshal their strength to develop multiple inputs into the decision making process. At that point it might become quite unnecessary. But in a sense, what this has done is to focus a good part of our discussion here today and a good part of the discussion in Congress, as well as in other places, on the Delaney amendment. This may very well be one of those forms of random noise to which I alluded.

I think that we really have to worry about how we develop responsibly the kind of adversarial proceedings that will indeed take cognizance of consumer as well as industrial and scientific interests. Hopefully, that is toward what this Forum is at least a small step.

HOGNESS: Thank you. Dr. Long?

FRANKLIN A. LONG: Someone referred to us over here during the day as the scientists. I looked myself up and, sure enough, I am there as a chemist. I have to confess that as I have listened today, I feel very much more like a member of the lay public or a member of the consumer group, because the particular field under discussion is one that is a little remote from the kind of chemistry I practiced.

I found myself, over and over again, being interested not so much in what scientists would do specifically, technically, but much more in how they would interact with the rest of the people involved in policy making and how their input too could be brought in early on in the decision making in an interactive way. Someone made the comment that the scientists were perhaps being put out in left field. I am not really at all troubled about being in left field as long as we are continued in our proper place in the batting order.

The other thing that I gave some thought to was this question of what is the role of outsiders? Much of our discussion has concerned how the FDA does its job? That is the insider group. I think that Joshua Lederberg is right in that this should be a much more pluralistic activity. There really are some important roles for outside groups. At one extreme are the pure consumer groups that come in with pronounced skepticism. At the other extreme are the closely linked advisory groups. I do think, however, that there is a place for serious independent study efforts relating very much to these problems. I, myself, would like to see the medical profession, especially the medical schools, take a much more active role in what I would call applied work in, among other things, bringing this problem of drug efficacy and safety in with the rest of the public health problem. It seems to me that there has been that curious one-sidedness about our discussion. We have been focusing very heavily on drugs.

In thinking about what is the role of these independent outside study groups, the fact that I believe they are necessary and highly desirable does not mean that I am automatically critical of the FDA. It is simply that it, too, is a bureaucracy with a certain number of bureaucratic characteristics interacting with other bureaucracies. The analogy that I thought of is the one of the role that outside groups played in the discussion and debate on the anti-ballistic missile system. Outsiders, I think, were really very important here -- knowledgeable, expert outsiders -- not that they had brand new ideas, but in some measure they could neutralize the position of the Defense Department in saying that all knowledge starts with them and ends with them. It seems to me that too can be the useful role of outside groups vis a vis the FDA, and I strongly hope that the medical schools and the rest of us take this up.
DR. HOGNESS: Thank you. Dr. Morrison?

PHILIP MORRISON: I would like to pick up on that. I am still a less biologically oriented member of the panel than a physical chemist. As an astronomer, I have very little to say about these matters directly. But one thing that occurs to me is that there is something structurally wrong with the organization of the American scientific community, and especially the American medical community.

I do not mean to say that this is venal or deliberate. Yet looking back over a long day, in which I have learned a great deal, I see a lack. I do not think that you can criticize an operation as complex as this which touches the problems of democracy, the problem of equality of men before the law, along with technical problems of the most elaborate sort solely from one position on the team or solely from left field or right field, for that matter.

I think that if the academic and scientific communities are to make a really substantial input, they must develop structures that, while not in any large way, recapitulate the government agency and the industry, which we now see as free agents in this affair. It seems to me that we could have some small models, each with its own control.

I suppose there are a few dozen substantial medical schools. I could easily see one-third or one-fourth of one -- a fairly substantial group of people, probably like a very small pharmaceutical firm in capital size and housing -- undertake the task of producing, testing, marketing, getting public acceptance for a new drug in a small area, possibly to a specialized group of users. I do not know what the problems would be in something of this kind, in setting up an engineering style of some sort. It would at least break down the invariable association that nobody has done anything, nobody has met a payroll, nobody has put the label on the bottle except people about whose detachment one is upset. It seems to me that we have got to break down this structural differentiation; it can be done. I think that a yardstick style could be very well adopted.

HOGNESS: Thank you. It is now time to turn the podium back to Dr. Handler who has the simplest of all tasks in summarizing the entire discussion.

PHILIP HANDLER: The Panel for Inquiry has done a remarkable job of summarizing my own impressions in the course of the day.

Dr. Adams spoke of the need for a social invention. I hope that this Forum is the beginning of such an invention. We have been concerned with the process of regulating the introduction and use of chemical entities in our society, the mechanisms by which we may see to it that we introduce those which we desire and reject those which should be avoided. This intrinsically difficult process has been evolving for a long time. Someone pointed out today how far we have come. Obviously, the more sophisticated we become, the more penetrating our questions, and the higher our expectations in these regards. This is but one aspect of our "ever floating aspirations," of man's perennial desire to improve on his current state.

Mr. Hutt spoke of the inevitable denouement in the regulatory process. After the regulatory agency has made a decision, someone will object, either the affected industry or the consumer. The matter, in turn, will wind up in the courts. There we will have the attorney for one side arguing with the attorney for the other before a third attorney, the judge. Instinctively, perhaps, I find such an arrangement very troublesome. And yet as I read decisions in these cases, I find them remarkably good. I do not quite understand how it occurs, but I have read numbers of such decision papers and find them astonishingly incisive and understanding of what is at stake. This, it seems to me, is part of the great genius of the American governmental system.

There might, however, be great utility in some intermediary process, in a special referee interposed between the regulatory agency and the need to go to the courts; if nothing else, such an agent could serve in the role of amicus curiae for the court. This Academy has so served in several instances; indeed, we are expected to do so in rather specific instances by the terms of several statutes. But a more general invention is not available.

In the total flow of current decision making, the consumer interest has by far the best opportunity for its representation at the level of the courts. Whether or not an equal opportunity can be made available earlier in the decision process is open to exploration. It seems clear that at all times the process should include consumer representation, as I understand the meaning of the term. Such representation is certainly to be welcomed, and I am sure that, in the course of time, Mr. Hutt and his colleagues will learn how to arrange this. A panel system would be a difficult process. As was pointed out, this has the peculiar property that the individuals in question now arrive "wearing their lab coats" as scientists and supposedly "objective," but those scientists representing consumer groups may very well be the only "advocates" on such panels.

In our own experience at the Academy, in managing several hundreds of committees at any one time, we go to extraordinary lengths to establish objective bodies. If on a given committee we have one known advocate, we make sure that he is balanced by others representing all the corners that may be involved in the problem. If we can, we prefer to have no advocates whatever. But true objectivity must be a rare commodity. Accordingly, a panel system that allows for a special advocate (the so-called consumer interest) and asks neutrality of all the others is a system I do not quite understand.

Most importantly, it seems to me from what I heard today, full and free communication is of the essence. Communication undoubtedly has been inadequate over

the years. At the moment, the various parties to these conversations are only
beginning to learn how to talk to each other. If we can continue to do so with a
minimum of animus, as here today, I think that experiences such as this, and many
others here and elsewhere, will well serve the national interest.

As a case in point, I note that Mr. Turner's exposition of his understanding
of the Delaney clause was certainly nothing like any ideas that I have previously
heard expressed. Dr. Wescoe's description of his relationship to that clause was,
I think, a rather fair representation of how most of the pharmaceutical industry
reacts to it. Mr. Hutt told us that, in point of fact, the Delaney clause has
been invoked only two times. I share Mr. Snodgrass's surprise that it had not
been invoked in the case of cyclamates. This may be taken as a demonstration of
our communicative failure; evidently we need many other forums and places in
which to talk and attempt to reduce our misunderstandings.

Withal, the system will still have to operate as a set of a continuing
tensions. The only institutions in our society for producing new drugs, at the
moment, are the pharmaceutical houses; their motivation is profit. Profit is
not an ugly term in American society. The drive for profit is the way that most
of this society gets on with its business -- in the broader sense of that word.
Laboratories seek to produce new chemical entities in the hope that they will find
useful places in American medicine, in the food industry, and in other sectors.
If the laboratories fail in this effort, it is the stockholders who have to pay
the bill. If they succeed, then, happily, both the stockholders and the public-
at-large benefit from the process. That, at least, should be the philosophy;
I suspect that it is in most cases. As long as that be true, the companies will
advance their causes, and there will remain the necessity for the FDA, or something like the FDA, to serve the society as it now attempts to do. And the courts

must provide opportunity for all voices to be heard before final decisions are actually taken.

Learning how to improve on that process is not easy. I doubt that we manage other sets of opposing tensions in our national life significantly better. It should not be surprising that we do not yet manage this one very well, but we should go right on trying.

Finally, I would like to say that during the day I repeatedly sensed a difference between the people whom I would call "scientists," and those I thought of as not being specifically scientists. These groups really do think differently, as I heard them. There was frequent mention of the risk-benefit equation, but it was not used the same way by both groups. The nonscientists who talked about safety seemed to mean absolute safety while they really were not very willing to consider benefits as an offset. The scientists who spoke about risks were quite willing to think about sufficient benefits as an offset. This is quite a different attitude. I guess it was Joshua Lederberg who said that the onus lies with the FDA to provide some guidelines. I am sure that FDA will shy away from this if they possibly can avoid having to come to grips with the question. Hence, we will continue to address every one of these instances in ad hoc fashion. Certainly any generally formulated guidelines would be smashed as soon as they are produced.

The Delaney clause was discussed in several ways. I am pleased that it did not become the focus of this day's discussion. For my part, I begin to view that clause as a great red herring rather than as a problem in our society. Certainly, on its face, all other things being equal, it is a perfectly rational guide to desirable societal behavior. No one in his right mind wants to put carcinogens into anything intended for human consumption. We should be perfectly willing to accept that guideline until the day when we find ourselves in the position of banning as a carcinogen some chemical entity which also offers great benefit. Until that time comes, we will not have to test the validity of the Delaney principle. When it does, we will have no recourse but to test the validity of the principle in a real life situation.

Meanwhile, talking about a problem that is nonexistent in reality does not serve our purposes particularly well. It has been said that the great harm of the Delaney clause is its deterrence to those who might otherwise be exploring new and important food additives. No such real case in point is known to me. I agree that one must be troubled by a law that, in effect, seems to say: "Since Compound X has been shown to be tumorigenic in high doses, go no further; do not look at the lower end of the dose-response curve, regardless of benefit." Such a situation seems, to me, to be repugnant. But the time to address it will be the day when a real test case is before us.

Finally, then, I would like to thank all of you who spent the day with us. I hope that some of you have found this as useful an experience as we have in respect to the specific responsibilities of the National Academy of Sciences. We hope that we also have served the nation in providing this opportunity for a very complex discussion to which you have all contributed so well.

OVERVIEW

Daniel E. Koshland, Jr.

Probability versus certainty, speed versus caution, the present versus the future--all of these polarities are present in the design of policy on drugs and food additives. Moreover, the extraordinarily complex assessment of benefits and risks that must be made for any one drug or food additive inevitably is dwarfed within the larger framework of all the contingencies of policy relating to it. The evaluation of individual cases and the grand sweep of policy emerged as a central issue in the first Academy Forum.

The title "How Safe Is Safe?" -- or perhaps more accurately "How Safe Is Safe Enough?" -- anticipated that issue. The word safe has different meanings for different people, and the Forum discussion revealed the wide range of emotional reaction to it. The consumer representative, concerned with the safety of individuals consuming a new drug or food additive, would like to be "certain" that it is "safe." The scientist decries "certainty" and replies that all life is "probability." In actuality, consumer advocates know that absolute safety is impossible, and scientists recognize that probability cannot eliminate the need for a legal definition of safe. Although absolute safety could be approached, it would be with enormous expense and delay. Considering the economic complexities of our society, extraordinary expense devoted to the development of a drug would inevitably lead to neglect of other critical considerations such as traffic, crime, and transportation. Design of policy in any one area, therefore, must involve assessments of probabilities which somehow put into reasonable balance the benefits, the risks, the expenses, the delays in relation to all such contingencies in other areas.

The participants in this Forum were sophisticated individuals, most of whom have contributed significantly to the development and/or legal control of drugs and food additives. Many of the differing adversary positions were known in advance. It was not surprising, therefore, to witness the opposing stances of consumer groups and industry. However, as the proceedings are examined in retrospect, several fundamentally different philosophies emerged which were not entirely obvious before and need to be considered seriously in the design of future policy. One of these seems to be the difference in reference points of the science and consumer groups, a variance which was more basic than their divergent judgments of actual risks and benefits. Scientists are emotionally identified with the future and the statistical individual, whereas consumer groups are emotionally identified with the present and the living individual.

Scientists are well aware that humans are not guinea pigs, and consumer groups know that an individual case cannot decide a policy. Yet the scientist is inevitably designing inventions or cures or concepts for future use. He is thus dealing with individuals who are yet unborn, whose faces have not yet become visible, individuals who are statistics without names or street addresses. Consumer groups, on the other hand, have another perspective. Their clients are living people; they wish to correct current abuses; they are frequently dealing with individuals whom they have seen or at least have learned about from reading a case history.

These viewpoints lead to an inevitable bias in the assessment of risks and benefits to the society. To the scientist, the number of individuals who might benefit in future generations is so much greater than the number who suffer risk in any chemical drug trial that he can easily bow to the tyranny of numbers and react impatiently to conservative controls. To the consumer advocate, the tears of one individual or the tragedy of a single crippled body are so much more compelling than statistics that he can easily forget the perils of delaying a drug. The two groups have spokesmen who are equally dedicated, intelligent, and moral. These men of good will differ not because they are perverse, but because the deep philosophical bases of their commitments are quite different.

This difference in basic commitment was reflected in other fundamental groups participating in the Forum. The industrialist starts with the bias of wanting to see a new drug or new product developed. He accepts the need for control, but he wants to get on with the job. He is impatient with delay and would like laws with greater emphasis on creativity and less on safety. The legislator tends to be in the middle, between consumer and producer, but with another bias, the need to operate in the political arena. In that situation the benefits to some individuals may be more important than benefits to others. The regulator has an even more complicated role with the need to make decisions based on science as he keeps an eye toward politics and on a time scale which often cannot allow for time consuming data collection. The different viewpoints became particularly apparent in the Forum discussion because the adversary positions were stated in an atmosphere which was optimal for constructive and rational debate. The heat of polemic confrontations was avoided, and yet it was still clear that the philosophical gaps were wide.

An illustration of these difficulties came out in the complaint by James Turner in regard to the 260 cases of illness associated with defective polio vaccine, 10 of which resulted in death. The scientist looking at the overall Salk polio program can easily ridicule these figures because the number of individuals saved in future generations is so enormously greater than this small number of unfortunate victims. If the purely statistical attitude is taken, however, one can conclude that any field trial of an ultimately successful drug, no matter how sloppily conducted, will always be offset by future gain. Does this logic allow the designer of tests to ignore the hazards to the living in order to protect future generations? Quite clearly not, and dialogue between widely divergent value systems is going to be necessary in order to design policy effectively in this area.

Another important problem to be illuminated was the gap between the written law and the implementation of that law. Although the Delaney clause was not the single concern of the Forum, it clearly depicted the difficulties in designing a law. It came as a revelation to many that the Delaney clause has been invoked only infrequently. The clause serves as a gray eminence to many Food and Drug Administration decisions and is the focus of much debate in the press. The absolute nature of its language has been ridiculed by the scientist. Its virtues in reversing what they consider to be industry-oriented decisions have been extolled by consumer groups. The Forum's invited discussants left the impression that the language of the amendment is imprecise, that it would some day have to be changed, and that yet it so far has not been invoked erroneously. Moreover, it has a strength of language which its predecessors lack. It was readily agreed that in the not-too-distant future some chemical possibly present in mother's milk will be shown to "cause cancer in experimental animals." Yet the defenders of the clause point out that its qualifying phrase stating "in an appropriately defined scientific test" validates its proper usage. This escape hatch can allow men of good judgment to avoid invoking the Delaney clause in an obviously absurd situation.

The flaws in such a situation are obvious, and yet the discussion emphasized the difficulty in writing laws involving science when a final scientific assessment is not available. Laws on science can probably never be written precisely unless they cover a highly specialized situation. If the language is detailed but avoids subjective judgments, it can be ridiculed by objective scientific fact. If it is too loosely worded, it can become a device for the protection of privilege or the cloak for excessive vigilantism. The nature of scientific policy requires a moderately precise law administered by individuals who wish to preserve the spirit of the law. The atmosphere in which the protagonists of various viewpoints meet to evaluate their different philosophies, therefore, will be essential for the design of legal wordings and perhaps most importantly for effective administration. The angry confrontations in the media and at congressional hearings or the expected platitudes before societies of the already converted can serve valuable purposes on occasion. At other times they can be self-defeating and obstructive. A meeting of adversaries in the disciplined environment offered by the Forum may well be an essential instrument for continuing the evaluation and design of scientific policy. The men who design laws will have to live with those who administer them, and gatherings of the sort exemplified in this discussion will provide a modus vivendi for continuous dialogue.

The extraordinarily difficult role of the regulator became apparent in the assessment of his role. Not only must he evaluate benefits and risks that are frequently hard to ascertain at all, he must work within the confines of political time. In highly complex decisions, such as those on cyclamate, diethylstilbesterol, and red dye, it is not possible for the FDA to wait for the completion of scientific tests. In fact the appropriate scientific tests may take years, and even then they may not be definitive. The FDA decision must be made if not tomorrow at least by the end of the current legislative session. The assessment of benefits and risks under this situation must be made by earnest men with humility and rationality.

The idea that certain procedures are "safe" and other procedures "defective" emerged in the Forum as an oversimplified conclusion. The banning of cyclamates regarded by some as a victory for morality was probably in fact nothing of the sort. It may indeed have been a great victory for practicality, i.e., with the fragmentary scientific data available the risk of cancer from cyclamates may be greater than the benefits of reduced obesity or pleasant taste. But the basis for that scientific conclusion is extraordinarily fragile.

As Joshua Lederberg pointed out, the extrapolation from animal to human experiments is far from perfect. We do not even know the nature of the curve, whether there is a threshold phenomena, whether there is a linear extrapolation, or whether there is a particularly susceptible group of individuals. Yet we are talking about enormous numbers even in the United States with only a fraction of the world population. Philip Handler pointed out that a risk of 1 part in 10^6 in a population of 200 million people means 200 victims. Can we demand that the probability of danger be reduced to 1 part in 10^8? If so, no drug or additive may ever satisfy such a stringent requirement. Yet on the other hand, can we accept 1 part in 10^4, a finding which would mean 20,000 victims in the continental United States alone?

Quite clearly the acceptable benefit-risk ratio alters as we consider the severity of an illness against those whom we are protecting. Dr. Lederberg pointed out that the Delaney clause puts an infinite value on avoiding cancer. If one then assigns other diseases, such as obesity, some other quantitative factor, the equation can then become extraordinarily complicated. Since we cannot truly extrapolate from animal experiments to assess the risk of cancer accurately, it becomes even more difficult to balance several imprecise benefits against several imprecise risks.

The need to expand our knowledge to carry out basic research in animal and human life processes was underscored repeatedly in the Forum as a necessity for both new drugs and new policies. As drugs for most of the common, large-scale killer diseases are being uncovered, the future may need complex drugs for diseases which strike a smaller fraction of the population. Since the financial reward from such drugs may be limited, industrial developers will need a high plateau of basic research to make the final applied push to the summit financially possible. Perhaps we will have to start educating the public for the "$1,000 pill" envisaged by Dr. Lederberg.

Basic research also can provide a more rational extrapolation from animal experiments to human responses. Dr. Lowry pointed out that we do not still know the detailed metabolic consequences of most of our more successful drugs, medicines which have been used for years. The massive field trials on one drug that gives a small hopeful sign become increasingly expensive as the need for safety is emphasized and controls become more stringent. What is needed is a fundamental understanding of the way in which metabolic reactions can be extrapolated from experimental animals to man. This basic knowledge would then allow most of the testing to be done inexpensively on small experimental animals so that the field trials on humans would be largely predictable. Such a development would not only expedite the appearance of new drugs but would provide a more scientific basis for regulation.

The design of policy quite clearly involves more than scientists. Lawyers, economists, and politicians are demanding a say in what used to be technical expertise. Since most of the issues are what Alvin Weinberg calls trans-scientific, the argument to leave scientific decisions to the scientist has little appeal. Consumer representatives are demanding that they be placed on committees which in the past have been considered largely scientific. This demand is resisted by scientists who argue: "Let us assess the data objectively, and the public can then place the value judgments." Mr. Turner, arguing for the consumer, stated that the consumer groups need to be part of the policy design process since the experiments can be influenced by the bias of the investigator and the stringency of controls also subtly shaped by philosophical principles.

From the other side, industry is concerned about shifting guidelines. Dr. Burns pointed out that industry would like nothing better than to be told simple rules to get a drug accepted. In practice, however, it is found that the ground rules may change even during the time interval in which the drug is being developed. The design of policy is not going to be a tidy affair in which the inputs from various groups can be neatly outlined on a chart. Scientists and laymen are going to have to learn to work with each other and to accept a new language of trans-science.

The issues of risk-benefit discussed in this Academy Forum differ in detail, but not in principle, from the issues of risk and benefit in many other areas of our society. Our energy resources, for example, require policy on the development of high-risk sources, such as nuclear energy, which are immediately available or on low-risk sources, such as solar energy, which may be inadequate. Pollution controls can bring benefits to cities through smog control devices but may impose costs on rural areas which have no need for such devices. It might seem that the general problem can be solved easily by simply assessing the risks and the benefits, and by going ahead only when the benefits outweigh the risks. But the Forum revealed that it is not easy to find a common denominator for risks and benefits. Further, it is not at all clear that the people who suffer the risks are likely to reap the benefits.

The choices to be made may constitute complex multiple factors; the risk of death, the psychological risk of eating unattractive food for a prolonged period, the risk of crippling, the risk of economic deprivation, the risk of avoiding cancer, the risk of children with genetic defects.

Although the Forum illustrated abundantly that these problems cannot be solved by science alone, it also made clear that they cannot be solved without the help of science. Unless scientific data and scientific principles are used to make some assessments of risks and benefits, there is no rational solution to the problems we face. The presentation of adversary positions in a climate of searching inquiry is perhaps one of the best for cutting to the core of the problem in an expeditious manner. It is hoped that the social device of the Forum process can serve a catalytic role in the design of better policies.

COMMENTARY

From: Harold M. Peck, M.D.
        Executive Director
        Department of Safety Assessment
        Merck Institute for Therapeutic Research
        West Point, Pennsylvania

It is unfortunate that this Forum did not include scientists immediately involved in interpreting and making judgments from the results of studies on drugs and food additives in the areas of pharmacology and toxicology in animals with the ultimate extrapolation of the results to the human. Clinicians experienced in initial clinical investigations as well as more extensive studies of drugs in man should have been included also. These are the individuals who, with the concurrence of regulatory agencies, must make the decisions on the potential value of new agents.

It is understandable that it would be desirable to have drugs and food additives which are completely safe. Conceptually this is an unattainable goal, and we must accept relatively safe for its proposed use or resort to therapeutic nihilism. I do not know of any chemical which cannot be shown to have some type of adverse effect if examined under appropriately rigorous conditions. This fact appears to be ignored by many individuals and certainly should be emphasized at some point in the series of your forums. It is altogether too easy to use adverse effects obtained in animals or in man under unusual or inappropriate conditions to condemn a chemical. Such a condemnation is a disservice to consumers whether related to the needless restrictions to therapeutic agents or to food additives, etc.

* * *

From: William Lijinsky
        Senior Scientist, Biology Division
        Oak Ridge National Laboratory
        Oak Ridge, Tennessee

I hope that the following may offer some clarification of matters discussed in the Forum.

A chemical is tested alone at high doses because the groups of animals used are small. The time of exposure is short relative to man because of the short lifespan of the experimental animals.

If the test is negative, as is usual, then the chemical can be accepted as non-carcinogenic. But, if the test is positive and cancer is induced, the chemical must be considered carcinogenic, and the Delaney clause applies.

The basis of a zero tolerance level for a carcinogenic chemical, even if the carcinogenic effect has been demonstrated at high dose levels, is that man never consumes such a chemical by itself. Its effect, though small, can be reinforced by hundreds (or possibly thousands) of small doses of other carcinogenic chemicals, and the total carcinogenic effect might be large enough to cause cancer in man.

* * *

From: Marsha N. Cohen
       Attorney
       Consumers Union
       Washington, D. C.

Almost at the end of the Forum, I noted that the day's discussions had neglected to consider the benefit side of the benefit-risk equation except in the area of drugs whose benefits were unquestioned. I asked the panelists how they rate and weigh the benefits of various food additives, especially colors, flavors, texturizers, and other primarily cosmetic additives.

Response to the query came from one discussant, Richard L. Hall, vice president, Research and Development, McCormick & Company, Inc. Mr. Hall stated that it is a flawed and false analysis to attempt to construct a hierarchy of values in regard to food additives because there are an infinite number of variables upon which consumers make their food choices.

I found this answer extremely distressing. It implied that no weighing of benefits would be reasonable, based upon what appears to be a theory that consumers should not be denied anything that might be a factor in their food choice. The logical counterpart to this argument would be the position -- which I doubt Mr. Hall takes -- that no weighing of risks is reasonable either, because consumers should not be denied anything that might be a factor in their food choice. This position, it seems to me, suggests that regulation is inherently suspect because it imposes value judgments. Yet the primary purpose of the Forum was to discuss just how policy makers should make those judgments which the law and a long regulatory history require them to make. To deny that food additives can be ranked in terms of relative benefits casts a smoke screen over a basic regulatory concern, although it makes a forceful debater's point, appreciated, as the applause indicated, by the food additive industry.

Perhaps I am naïve, but I cannot believe that informed citizens would consider that policy decision valid which exposed them to the same risk for the sake of a pleasant flavor or a pretty color as it did for the prevention of food-borne disease. The problem before the Forum, so I assumed, was how we, as scientists, consumers, and regulators, should weigh the many factors to be considered in deciding whether a food or a drug is safe enough for consumption, considering the potential benefits to the public. With all respect to Mr. Hall, his position that all food additives are equally beneficial ignores a difficulty central to this decision making process, and sounds more like industry rhetoric than scientific logic. Even the defense of FD&C Red No. 2, I submit, can rest on firmer ground.

* * *

From: Richard L. Hall
        Vice president, Research and Development
        McCormick & Company, Inc.
        Hunt Valley, Maryland

Ms. Cohen's question asked the benefits of colors, presumably meaning that these should be measured in order to balance them against any risks, and implying that perhaps the benefits of colors are less than those of preservatives or some more "important" category.

It is a temptation to set up a scale of values for different groups of additives, classified by technical effect and arranged in a hierarchy of what seems to be importance. But this is a superficial, simplistic, and deeply flawed exercise which collapses under the weight of critical and factual examination.

No single additive is indispensable. Each is exchangeable for one or usually more than one of the following: (1) another additive or additives; (2) a change in process; (3) an increase in cost; (4) a decrease in acceptability; (5) a loss of one or more products; or (6) some small, immeasurable increase in risk.

Obviously, some particular additive may be more important than another. But this importance relates little, if at all, to whether it is a preservative, a nutrient, or a color. Importance, instead, depends on whether the additive is easily replaceable, and at what cost.

We could do without the sulfites; but some dehydrated fruits and vegetables would be less attractive and taste less good. Others would disappear altogether. Wine would be lower and more erratic in quality as well as more expensive.

We could do without all preservatives and without significant increase in vital risks; but the consequences would include a substantial loss of variety. To mention only a few, a number of cheeses -- including the most economical ones -- would disappear; so also would many more dried fruits and vegetables, bottled soft drinks, and fruit-based beverages, and many baked goods. Those that were left would keep less well and be more expensive.

We could do without added nutrients and yet not suffer malnutrition if we would pay more money, lose considerable variety, and eat what someone else prescribes as the "right" things. But that is not the way we ever have chosen, or ever will choose, our diets for long. Eating is more than an inconvenient biological necessity; it is a social activity, a cultural expression, and often a personal aesthetic experience.

The subjective factors -- flavor, texture, color, mouth feel, temperature -- in food choices are enormously varied and complex. They overwhelm what an outside observer would consider rational factors such as nutrition, safety, or even economics. But those aware of the physiological effects of flavor and odor perception and familiar with disorders such as dysgeusia and ageusia know these organoleptic factors have not only psychological, but decisive physiological effects on digestion and nutritional state. Unfortunately, we all find it easy to be cavalier about others' food preferences and very resentful of any effort to change our own.

What makes the risk-benefit exercise almost entirely inapplicable to foods is, first, that none of us in this affluent society wish or should have to accept any significant vital risk in our food. We do accept some; many of us eat too much salt, sugar, or saturated fat. But these risks are voluntary and individual; we do not have to accept them. What we do is another broad subject, and one of the reasons is the importance of flavor and texture in food choices.

Of course, not even in food can there be zero risk, but it is at a level so low that we do not with present knowledge consider it significant. What residues of vital risk there now are in our food supply are there because we do not know enough to detect, define, and eliminate them, not because we willingly accept them in exchange for certain non-vital benefits. Doubtless the day will come when we can define the nature and probability of some very remote vital risk with sufficient confidence to decide if it should continue to be available because of the associated non-vital benefits. This will raise many interesting ethical, legal, and economic questions. Will we then label some foods as we now do cigarettes? But for the present, food should be practically free of all vital risk -- certainly any that can be detected, defined, and eliminated. That being the case, one side of the risk-benefit "balance" is virtually empty, and the need to try to measure benefits as one would with a dangerous but life-saving drug is absent.

This is fortunate because risk-benefit analysis of food ingredients is also impossible, since food, although it is a continuing necessity, is not usually a vital benefit. Unless we are starving, and few of us are, it does not "contribute to an improvement in condition" (the definition of a benefit) in a vital way, as does a needed medicine. Thus we cannot, and should not, knowingly accept with our food any vital risks unless they appear so remote or small in importance as to be really negligible.

In summary, this is a complex set of interrelated considerations where there is an almost infinite opportunity for trade-offs among non-vital risks and benefits -- cost, convenience, pleasure -- but where there would be no general agreement among individuals on what those trade-offs should be. We serve the consumer best by recognizing this diversity of taste and need, and by providing the widest possible variety of choice to meet it. Within this variety we can by innovative processing and skillful regulation build into a high probability of adequate nutrition and the practical certainty of freedom from harm. But we cannot absolutely guarantee it. The more we restrict choice by imposing an unrealistic and absolutist view of nutritional value or of safety, or by imposing a hierarchy of needs based on our personal views of what is important in food, the greater the risk that consumer choices will break out of these restraints in ways that are unpredictable, unregulated, and uninformed. A regulated marketplace, not administrative fiat or elitist prescription, is the best server of consumer needs.

* * *

From: Herbert L. Ley, Jr., M.D.
Medical Consultant
Bethesda, Maryland

In addition to the need to inform the general public regarding the issues involved in the discussions of this Forum, I believe that it is also important that the academic medical community should be informed as well. This belief is based on the results of a survey which I personally conducted in April 1973. Although the results of the survey are being prepared for publication, I think it appropriate to comment that in 164 responses to 376 questionnaires mailed to professors of medicine, pediatrics, pharmacology, and biochemistry in the medical schools of the United States, 74 individuals (or 45% of those responding) indicated that they had no knowledge regarding the Delaney clause.

If the academic medical community is to play an active role in the public discussions of the issues of this Forum, it must be better informed.

* * *

From: Hans H. Landsberg
           Director, Resource Appraisal Program
           Resources for the Future, Inc.
           Washington, D. C.

I came away from the Forum on food additives and drugs with a series of questions.

My principal question might be formulated like this: If the Food and Drug Administration were staffed and operated to the satisfaction of all concerned (a wholly unrealistic supposition I admit!), what criteria would it apply to decide upon the release of a given substance? What data would it want (whether or not now available), and what information would be supplied to the various categories involved in the process (final consumers, doctors, hospitals, manufacturers, etc.)?

Since information has a price tag, how far is the process worth carrying? Dr. Lederberg attempted to answer this with one of his graphs in a proper theoretical fashion (I say _proper_ perhaps because it utilized an approach familiar to economists, i.e., marginal analysis). Yet neither he nor anyone else carried this approach to the next phase, i.e., what data one might use to locate the cut-off-point, i.e., the point where costs of information exceed expected benefits from it. Obviously, the more we worry about "safety" the less resources we have for other undertakings. Mortality statistics over the last few years, in the aggregate and in detail, make one at least hesitate as to whether we are worrying about the right things. I must confess my disappointment that apart from Dr. Handler's opening remarks and Dr. Lederberg's paper the central issue that I had anticipated would dominate the Forum was simply forgotten in the much less fruitful debate over the merits and demerits, and especially the latter, of the Food and Drug Administration.

Another question I would have liked to raise takes its cue from the term _policy_ _design_ in the Forum's title. There are, to my mind, several policies we should discuss, all in relation to safety:

(1) toward research process

(2) toward the private manufacturer

(3) toward the consumer

(4) toward the intermediary, i.e., the health profession --
     doctors, hospitals, etc.

In each instance, one would want to think of safety, and of the role of government especially, in different terms.

The discussion also would benefit from a distinction between individual health (and safety) and genetic or generic health (and safety). Which is at risk is important, and the location of responsibility shifts heavily, it seems to me, from individual to government in the "generic" case. After all, there are probably enough drugs -- and other products -- in the average American's home to kill himself by ingestion or otherwise if he is so inclined. He is given sufficient information to put him in a position not to harm himself, and that is the end of it. The government feels no obligation to go beyond the supply of information. Where health impact goes beyond the individual, the government's role should probably be a more forceful one. Another way of looking at it is that individuals will do their own discounting and odds-making, but only the government can perform that function where generic/genetic damage is involved.

Pertinent to policy design vis-à-vis the manufacturer are considerations having to do with credibility of safety-connected statements. Only recently has much attention been paid to assessing "effectiveness" of drugs. In their efforts at product differentiation (Is Bufferin better than Excedrin than Anacin

than Bayer's Aspirin than Salicylic Acid?) and excessiveness of claims, producers are putting at risk their credibility. In any policy designed to enhance
safety it would seem wise not to neglect the impact of factors such as the above.

A final question, probably as difficult to push toward a practical answer, is this: How can one approach the measurement of costs of safety in a
broader context that evaluates the alternatives and implications? For example,
if, as seems likely, the banning of DES and the consequent loss of feed-efficiency
necessitates the raising of more animals, the consumption of more grain, the use
of more fertilizer and pesticides, the reduced availability of food for the mal-
nourished, etc., etc., at what point do we cut off the evaluation and call it a
day, knowing that the addition -- or omission -- of one more link in the chain
may change the net balance?

These are some of the questions I would like to have seen tackled at the
Forum, even though I would have expected only marginal progress. With the odds
miniscule of getting an all-wise, all-loved FDA (or, for that matter, any other
regulatory agency) I'd take my chances at an Academy gathering for learning something more fruitful in the long run.

Lest I be misunderstood, in my single intervention at the Forum, I suggested
that the government "buy out" a manufacturer who could not afford to have warnings posted on his product. I did not, of course, mean to buy out the firm but
merely the right to market the product in question.

* * *

From: M. R. Clarkson, D.V.M.
      Peterborough, New Hampshire

It was disturbing to hear a Forum speaker assert that there is no public representation in Food and Drug Administration decision making, and state that action is necessary to change the situation by bringing in various groups to represent segments of the public.

Of course it is appropriate for the FDA to give all individuals and groups opportunity to be heard. That is the reason for the procedures outlined in the Administrative Procedures Act. It also is the reason for the procedural measures so ably outlined by Mr. Hutt.

But let us not forget that in adopting food and drug legislation -- beginning with the 1906 Act and continuing to the present -- the Congress has made it abundantly clear that the FDA is itself to represent the public, meaning all of the people all of the time regardless of the special interests of the many groups that may, or may not, appear on a particular issue.

This is the only way the system can work. Let us all bend our efforts to assist FDA in its continuing struggle to meet this responsibility.

* * *

From: W. Clarke Wescoe, M.D.
       Vice Chairman of the Board
       Sterling Drug, Inc.
       New York, New York

As is often the case, the Forum left me with a sense of disappointment, despite the careful attention that had characterized its planning. It is appropriate, therefore, to add a few comments.

Nowhere in the presentations or in the background information was any delineation made of the difficult task of drug discovery. I am afraid that the impression might be left that drug discovery is a haphazard exercise -- something the cognoscenti know is far from the truth. There should have been some opportunity for the audience to know of the long, complicated, costly task of developing a new pharmaceutical product beginning at the chemists' bench, and, after intricate and careful investigation, ending in the therapeutic armamentarium. I had the distinct impression that even some of those who made presentations were unaware of this process. The Forum missed a special opportunity to inform the public.

Regrettably, there were even those who implied inaccurate data and that unreliable investigators were common to pharmaceutical research. Such scurrilous comments reveal a regrettable lack of knowledge, an unfortunate attitude toward the academic community, and a disbelief in the integrity of science and those who practice it. The Food, Drug, and Cosmetic Act specifically states criminal, not civil, penalties for infractions. It serves no purpose to make unsubstantiated statements and, in fact, it does violence to the entire concept of the Forum, which I thought was to be a search for truth.

Unfortunately, the format of the Forum tended to perpetuate stereotypes -- to imply that industry, consumers, the academic world, and the regulatory agency must, of necessity, be adversaries. In my presentation, I attempted to dispel that myth. In retrospect, I was unsuccessful; and in retrospect, as well, it would appear that no one else cared to point out that in the specific area of pharmaceutical development there is an intersection of interest on the part of the regulatory agency, the academic community, the medical profession, and industry -- all in the long-term interest of the consumer.

Each of us is a consumer. Each of us has interest only in truth, only in products that are safe and effective. But safety is an elusive thing -- it is always a relative matter. And effectiveness, in certain clinical areas, cannot really be measured objectively; it remains, in analgesia for instance, a subjective matter.

I have in my lifetime experienced the stultifying effect of stereotypy. When I became a medical school dean, my professorial colleagues looked upon me in a little different light. When I became a university chancellor, there was even a subtle change in my relationships with my fellow deans (on their part, not mine). When I left the academic world for a place in the pharmaceutical industry, a similar change occurred. These changes defy my understanding, for I recognize in myself the same person regardless of my status. With no change in position has there been a change in my ideals, my knowledge, or my approach to problems. All that I see as change in myself is a few more "frown lines" and a little more weight around the waist. I would hope that in future Forums a determined attempt would be made to avoid stereotypy.

Finally, let me express my feeling about corporate responsibility in a paraphrase of the words of Dr. J. Mark Hiebert, chairman of the Board of my company: We work all day in such a way that we can sleep easily all through the night. That, so far as I am concerned, is an acceptable credo for any man, regardless of his profession.

* * *

FROM: James S. Turner
          Co-Director
          Consumer Action for Improved
           Food and Drugs
          Washington, D.C.

TO: W. Clarke Wescoe, M.D.
          Vice Chairman
          Sterling Drug Company, Inc.
          New York, New York

During the discussion of the Academy Forum on drugs and food additives, I said that there were eight or ten "instances where drugs have gotten through foreign mechanisms and caused problems but did not get through here."

You responded, "Do you know those instances? I would like them in the record for the sake of accuracy. I do not like unsupported statements."

Since you were interested in the information, I thought I would write directly to you and then submit the letter for inclusion in the printed version of the Forum.

The New York Times of February 6, 1973, reported on the testimony of Dr. Henry E. Simmons, Director of the FDA's Bureau of Drugs, given the preceding day before the Subcommittee on Monopoly of the Senate Small Business Committee. The article, by Times science writer Harold M. Schmeck, reported that "Dr. Simmons cited more than

two dozen different drugs of various kinds that have been
marketed abroad, but never in this country, and that have
recently been shown to have important safety problems."

One example of the dangers faced by foreign drug
users, but not Americans, concerns a potent, highly concentrated aerosol spray for bronchial asthma. Dr. Simmons
called the use of this drug in Europe while it was banned
in the United States "one of the greatest recorded
therapeutic disasters in modern history." Its use caused
a seven-fold increase in asthma mortality in only 7 years
in England. This accounted for 7 percent of all deaths
in children 10 to 14 years of age and a total of 3,500
excess deaths.

Dr. Simmons also cited an "epidemic" of deaths from
primary pulmonary hypertension associated with an appetite
depressing drug which was marketed in Switzerland, Austria,
and Germany, but not in the United States. The FDA stopped
the clinical testing of the drug in 1968 because of the
hazard it presented to the test subjects. For your information and the record of the Academy Forum, I am enclosing
the list (which Dr. Simmons submitted to the Senate Committee) of twenty-five drugs currently marketed overseas
but either dropped from human trials or disapproved for
marketing in this country because of significant safety or
effectiveness problems. Three of them have been withdrawn
from foreign use.

USE-INDICATION	ANIMAL DATA	HUMAN DATA
1. INDs Discontinued or Terminated Because of Significant Questions of Safety or Efficacy		
Hypotensive	Abnormal liver function	Liver dysfunction 84% of cases studied 31% discontinued treatment
Antischistosomal	Mutagenic Question of teratogenicity, carcinogenicity	Liver toxicity
Antifungal—Antibacterial	Similar to compounds shown carcinogenic	Early clinical studies indicate it second best to marketed compound
Various Mild Psychophysiologic Symptoms	Adverse effects reproduction—3 species Pathology in dog—kidney, liver, lungs	Liver dysfunction, leucopenia Alopecia, Stevens-Johnson Syndrome
Antibiotic	Hepatotoxicity—dogs	Abnormal liver function
Tranquilizer	Hepatotoxicity—dogs Cleft palate—rats and mice Increase mortality—newborn	Liver dysfunction (43%) Higher incidence other adverse reactions
Tranquilizer	Altered sterol metabolism Teratogenic effects—mice Complex set of effects on rat reproduction	Altered sterol metabolism Several reports of lens opacities and icthyosis Extreme frequency other side effects
Coronary Vasodilator	Cataracts—dogs	
Mucolytic	Convulsions—incidence and frequency dose-related in dogs —Rats Possibility of cataracts—rats Increased incidence mammary tumors—rats	
2. INDs Never Submitted		
Antimicrobial—Urinary Tract Infection	May induce lymphoblastic leukemia—mice Mammary tumors—rats	
Antitussive	Bladder carcinogen—rat Bladder changes (probably carcinogen)—dog	
Antitrichomonal	Related to compound showing carcinogenicity Possible ovarian suppression and other effects on reproductive function	
3. Drugs Marketed in Countries Other Than U.S.—Later Withdrawn		
Anorexigenic	Number of questions re drug stability and animal studies	Primary pulmonary hypertension
Sedative—Hypnotic	Teratogenic—monkey (After reported in humans)	Phocomelia
Anti-inflammatory	G-I side effects	"G-I side effects and jaundice"
4. INDs Continued Active with Restrictions		
B—Adrenergic Blockers in Cardiac Indications	Structurally related compound deemed carcinogenic (lymphosarcomas). Advisory Committee (preclinical) recommended carcinogenicity studies in 2 species	Cardiology Advisory Committee recommended short term use in certain conditions only pending completion of carcinogenicity studies.
Coagulant	"Biliary hyperplasia—rat"	Hereditary angioneurotic edema is proposed study
Anticonvulsant (Marketed as hypnotic other countries)	G-I Bleeding, leukopenia—Bone marrow hypoplasia—teratogenic effects—suggestion liver, kidney alterations	Toxicity—liver dysfunction—hematopoietic Restricted to children with myoclonic seizures, infantile spasms, etc.
5. INDs Discontinued—No NDA		
Antidepressant	Narrow margin—lethality	Lethal dose calculated 4.5–6.5x Maximum recommended daily dose Convulsions—high daily dose
Anti-nausea		Studies completed—efficacious dose also produced high incidence extrapyramidal side effects
Anti-psychotic		Problems of study design, diagnostic criteria Results often contradictory
Anti-depressant		European studies indicate less effective than currently marketed compound.
6. IND/NDA Submitted not Approved		
Hypotensive		Questions of safety, efficacy, study design

One of the drugs listed, the antischistosomal drug which is the second drug in part one of the list, is of particular interest to our dialogue since it is manufactured by the Sterling Drug Company. I would be sincerely interested in hearing the reasoning behind the continued sale of this drug in underdeveloped sections of the world when a number of well-designed and well-conducted tests carried out by respected researchers established that it poses a serious hazard to the individuals who take the drug and to their offspring. Perhaps by tracing the argument behind the continued marketing of this drug by your company and the reasoning behind the critics of its use, we might be able to more clearly understand and therefore resolve some of the more important issues that separated us during the Academy Forum.

Let me add that I truely enjoyed our exchanges during the Forum and look forward to the opportunity to continue our dialogue.

* * * *

FROM: W. Clarke Wescoe, M.D.
         Vice Chairman
         Sterling Drug Inc.
         New York, New York

TO: James S. Turner
         Co-Director
         Consumer Action for Improved
          Food and Drugs
         Washington, D.C.

The reason that I asked you to clarify your comments was that I inherently am opposed to anyone making unsubstantiated statements in a public forum, for these comments ofttimes take on the appearance of unqualified truth and scientific accuracy although the basis for them may be very slim indeed. With that latter thought in mind, I would now proceed to "set the record straight."

I note that you consider as incontrovertible evidence for your far-reaching statement a report that appeared in the public press and not in any scientific journal. Further, that report concerned an appearance by a government official before a senatorial hearing, under which circumstances the statements he made could not be refuted by anyone.

For your information, Dr. Simmons's "testimony" has been refuted at length by C. Joseph Stetler, President of the Pharmaceutical Manufacturers' Association, for

inclusion in the <u>Congressional Record</u>. I see no reason
to ask that the Academy publish his lengthy letter in
this transcript, nor do I believe it should print the
one you submitted because it contains errors of fact.
Moreover, I am very much opposed to the reprinting of a
table which is lacking in definitive information and
which presents only one side of a question. To my
knowledge, identification of the drugs involved has
been requested by the President of the Pharmaceutical
Manufacturers Association but no identification has been
forthcoming.

It is difficult to comment upon such "information"
in a vacuum. The implication, however, that every case
cited represents a clear instance of failure from the
standpoint of safety or efficacy is misleading. Just
as misleading is the implication that withdrawal of
INDs was an action initiated by government to protect
consumers.

By deduction it is possible to identify some of the
drugs. Some were withdrawn by the sponsoring company
because they lacked real importance or significant improvement over marketed drugs. Animal toxicity is often
species specific and an example of drug metabolic pathways
different from those seen in man.

You ask specifically about our antischistosomal drug and, therefore, give me an opportunity to put to rest vicious statements about it made by bacterial geneticists, <u>not</u> before the company of their peers but in the public press. In my opinion such activity is reprehensible. Studies in bacteria and in cell systems are looked upon by those qualified as <u>test models</u> and not definitive in assessing activity in the mammalian organism. Experts consider the final test to be that performed in the intact animal. In the case of hycanthone, it is true that when it is exposed to a variant strain of <u>Salmonella typhimurium</u> it produces a mutation. What it does is to convert a mutant strain back to the normal strain. In medicine we would call that a cure! The definitive study in a well-substantiated strain of mice was performed under the direction of Dr. William L. Russell at the Oak Ridge National Laboratories. Those studies, which involved more than 16,000 mice, each evaluated at seven test loci, revealed that hycanthone produced <u>no</u> mutations. The scientists concluded that <u>if</u> hycanthone were to produce mutations it would be at a rate only 6 percent of the spontaneous frequency. The clinical dose of hycanthone is 3 mg/kg administered one time only. The mice were treated with 50 times that dose (150 mg/kg).

In what I consider an attempt to impress the public
(not science) with the value of bacterial genetics, the
bacterial geneticists continue to trumpet their findings
and ignore the massive work done in the definitive system recognized by all scientific bodies as the sine qua
non in scientific investigation. I need not remind you
that Dr. Russell is one of the world's authorities in
this field. He is the one who studied the effects of
ionizing radiation on genetic structures in the mammal.
May I suggest that you ask him to substantiate what I
have written. His work can be found in the Bulletin of
the Oak Ridge National Laboratories. His work indicates
as can none in bacteria or in cell systems that the drug
does not pose a mutagenic hazard in man. The same, incidentally, has been stated by the expert committee of
the World Health Organization.

Hycanthone is an effective drug in the treatment of
schistosomiasis produced by Mansoni or hematobium and as
safe as any drug in use, including tartar emetic. It is
unequivocally false that the IND on the antischistosomal
drug was terminated because of safety or toxicity questions.
The IND was discontinued because the necessary clinical
investigations involving sophisticated laboratory studies
were completed. No NDA was ever requested simply because
the drug is not manufactured in this country and because

schistosomiasis is not a problem in the United States,
a fact which I believe you know.

I object strenuously to your comment that isoproterenol,
the drug for bronchial asthma, "was banned" in the United
States. Nothing could be further from the truth: in fact,
that drug has been marketed in the United States for more
than thirty years and is the drug of choice today for the
treatment of asthma. The dosage form implicated in difficulties in England was never considered by any manufacturer
in the United States.

Beyond that, the evidence is not really clear that
the data quoted for the concentrated form in England reveal
the entire story. Saying that "one of the greatest recorded
therapeutic disasters in modern medical history" was averted
in this country because of FDA's standards, Dr. Simmons
cited the marketing in England of a high-dose aerosol
isoproterenol nebulizer for bronchial asthma as the direct
cause of a seven-fold increase in asthma mortality in that
country over a seven-year period. The fact is that it is
not known how many of the asthmatic patients who died in
England used the drug. Nor is the extent of use by
patients with chronic bronchitis known (the death rate
from bronchitis in England and Wales is at least ten times
greater than that for asthma alone); and asthma death
rates in Australia and Holland, for example, show no
significant change during the period, even though the

product's sales increased markedly in those countries.
Why did the English death rate multiply? The change may
at least partially be due to a 1957 change in the International Classification of Diseases, which separated the
statistics for "asthma" from "asthma with bronchitis."
The result was to produce an apparent reduction in deaths
from asthma, since "asthma with bronchitis" was excluded
from the asthma statistics. Thus the figure for asthma
mortality in England in 1959 and 1960 was the lowest one
reported by that country in thirty years. Even though
the figure rose sharply after 1960, it never reached much
more than half of the average rate between 1941 and 1950.
Moreover, the death rate from asthma rose in many nations
(Japan, Denmark, Sweden) where the product in question
was not available. At the very least, assertions about
this case represent a very selective use of unrepresentative
and misleading studies. They were used to construct a
therapeutic disaster which in fact may not have occurred,
and then gave the FDA credit for preventing it.

About the other compounds to which Dr. Simmons referred I have no intimate knowledge. I would like to say,
however, that it is not unusual for a company to withdraw
an IND when clinical investigation reveals a problem not
anticipated in animal studies or predictable from them.

I, too, enjoyed our exchanges at the Forum. I
believe, however, that the Forum failed, in part, because
it allowed too much rhetoric and insisted too little upon
concentrating on facts. Thank you for giving me the
opportunity to respond to you.

* * *

From: Samuel S. Epstein, M.D.
        Swetland Professor of Environmental Health
            and Human Ecology
        Case Western Reserve University Medical School
        Cleveland, Ohio

In discussions on socially acceptable risks, references have been made to problems of scientific evaluation, with particular emphasis on providing information critical to the development of a reasoned benefit-risk calculus. It is my view that the "safety" problems confronting us now are not largely scientific, but rather problems relating to the decision making process and to what reasonably may be regarded as the broad public interest.

It is abundantly clear that there are major defects in the federal decision making process in general, and in the regulatory process in particular. The system of checks and balances traditionally inherent in the democratic process is largely absent from current regulatory practice. Apart from limited post hoc recourse, citizens and consumers, as well as those who represent their interests scientifically and legally, are virtually excluded from involvement in vital decisions affecting the public-at-large. The concept of matching benefits against risks has been applied to maximize short-term benefits to industry even though this may entail minimal benefits, maximal risks, and externalized costs to the consumer. Such an approach is often detrimental and counterproductive to the long-term interest of industry, which may suffer major economic dislocation when hazardous products to which major commitments have been made are belatedly banned from commerce.

Such problems are, in a large measure, attributable to crippling constraints which have developed in the total regulatory process. Responsibility for such constraints, with specific reference to drugs and food additives, must be shared with the Food and Drug Administration, by the legislature, the scientific community, and by consumers and citizens who have not yet developed adequate mechanisms for protecting their own vital interests and rights.

Risks and specters with which we have been confronted are starvation of mankind, gross malnutrition, and disease, which largely have been prevented by the use of chemical additives and new drugs. No one, generally, has any argument against the use of additives and drugs that are efficacious and serve broadly useful societal functions. However, arguments arise when chemical products which are not efficacious and which do not serve broad and societally useful functions are marketed, and especially when the potential hazards of such chemicals are improperly assessed or even misrepresented.

THE BENEFIT-RISK CALCULUS

To understand the problem of benefit and risk evaluation, practical distinctions should be made between technological innovations and new chemical products which have not yet been built into commerce, for which it is possible to develop more restrictive regulatory approaches, and those chemical products which are already built into commerce, and for which major economic dislocations may ensue if restrictions are belatedly developed.

To evaluate the risk-benefit relationship, a critical data base is needed and this base relates to three primary components:

- The efficacy of the material. Does the product, drug, or food additive serve a useful purpose?

- What is the precise chemical identity of the product?

- Is the product safe?

Having stated the self-evident requirements for data on these three components -- efficacy, identity, and safety -- the next obvious question is, What are the quality of the data on which judgments may be properly based? It has gradually become self-apparent that certain critical data, relating to both safety and efficacy, submitted to regulatory agencies suffer from a variety of constraints that range in extremes from the manipulated and fraudulent to the inadequate or incompetent.

EFFICACY

Efficacy or effectiveness may be defined in two distinct ways. In the narrow Federal Trade Commission (FTC) sense of the term, it merely means that a product will achieve its stated objective. In other words, if a green or yellow Florida or Alabama orange is colored red with a synthetic dye, then this dye achieves its stated objective.

Many chemical products do not even satisfy requirements for this narrow definition of efficacy. A recent National Academy of Sciences task force report revealed that approximately 60 percent of the drugs evaluated were not effective (nonefficacious); this is in clear contravention of the 1962 Kefauver-Harris amendment to the Food, Drug, and Cosmetic Act. Until recently, the major use of DDT in the United States against DDT-resistant cotton pests constituted a similar example of nonefficacy, as did the use of monosodium glutamate as a flavor enhancer in baby foods.

The broader concept of efficacy, however, relates to the question of whether there are societal benefits attendant on the use of this product. Are there societal benefits to the massive use of cosmetic food additives for the purpose of making food appear more attractive, of better quality, and fresher than it really is? For instance, as far as nitrites are concerned -- excluding their important preservative function -- the major use of nitrites is to make meat look redder and fresher than it really is.

Distinctions should be made, even allowing for possible bias and special value judgments, between the narrow FTC sense of efficacy, in which products achieve their stated objective, and the broader concept of efficacy, in which such products are expected to serve a broadly useful societal purpose. Such purposes might be the preservation of food, making it available to large human populations, and also the curing or prevention of disease. It is the latter type of broad societal efficacy which is clearly important, and to which we should properly address ourselves in discussions on the risk-benefit calculus.

What benefits are there to society from cosmetic food additives in general, and what benefits are there to society from adding cyclamates and caffeine to soda pop which young children massively consume? What use is there in adding monosodium glutamate to baby foods when there is no evidence that babies preferentially discriminate in favor of flavored baby foods? So, when we talk about benefit, let us really be clear what we mean. Do we mean benefit to a narrow economic segment of the community that produces cosmetic food additives, or do we mean broad societal benefits?

IDENTITY

When we talk about identity, and this is the second important question, we are asking what exactly are the chemicals being added to our food? There are currently no rigid and comprehensive requirements for complete ingredient labeling and disclosure of identity. So the consumer does not know what additives are used in his food. In addition to the 600 or more compounds on the Generally Recognized As Safe (GRAS) list, and which have not been adequately evaluated for safety, the food industry also apparently has reserved for itself the right to

determine what other food additives are GRAS and thus exempt from safety testing.
The consumer thus cannot know exactly what additives are untested even if he did
know what additives were in his food.

The requirements for complete disclosure of identity are clearly critical
not only in relation to the parent chemical itself, but also for its contaminants,
pyrolytic, degradation, and metabolic products. For instance, with cyclamates
the major safety problem has not been with regard to cyclamate itself, but with
cyclohexylamine, its contaminant and metabolic product. Similarly, with the
class of phenoxy herbicides, the major public health problem basically has not
been with the herbicides themselves but with their dioxin contaminants and
pyrolytic products.

SAFETY

What is meant by safety, and why is there such concern on problems of
safety? This concern largely has occurred because there is growing realization
that much human disease is environmentally induced. There is a growing consensus
among leading cancer research workers that 60 to 80 percent of human cancer is
environmental in origin. So we are talking about real and major public health
issues, such as preventable cancer and birth defects, and not esoteric problems
of concern to an "extremist" few.

Evaluation of toxicity is developed in two ways: by testing in animals,
on an anticipatory basis; or by epidemiology, which means examining human populations to evaluate adverse effects on a post hoc basis. Sharp distinctions should
be made between toxicity per se, which is a reversible phenomenon and basically a
function of dose, and carcinogenicity, mutagenicity, and teratogenicity, which are
unique, specific, and irreversible phenomena.

Evaluation of carcinogenicity involves a set of special problems which are quite apart from the long latent period and from the difficulty in sometimes demonstrating causal relationships on an epidemiological basis. When chemicals are tested for carcinogenicity, mutagenicity, and teratogenicity, it is clear that routes of administration which reflect human exposure should be selected. It is also clear that more than one animal species should be tested.

In testing, one must accept the fact that toxicology is a grossly insensitive test system. Let us assume that you introduce into commerce an additive or drug which produces cancer or birth defects in one of every 10,000 humans. Let us also assume that the sensitivity of the rat or mouse to this additive or drug is the same as that of a human. You would then need 10,000 rats or 10,000 mice to get one cancer or one birth defect; for statistical significance, you may thus need to test 30,000 rats or 30,000 mice. In practice only 30 to 50 animals are used in a test group. So, therefore, if you test animals with levels at which humans are exposed, your chances of detecting carcinogenic, teratogenic, or mutagenic effects are virtually nil. In an attempt to reduce the gross insensitivity of the test system, a series of dosages which extend to the maximally tolerated should properly be used. The maximum tolerated dose means just that dosage which can be administered during the lifetime of an animal without inducing any weight loss or other overt evidence of toxicity.

Assumptions of equal sensitivity or similar sensitivity of rodents and humans are, of course, questionable. In some instances humans are more sensitive, and in others they are less sensitive, to the adverse effects of a particular chemical product. For example, aromatic amines produce cancer of the bladder in man, but not in mice or rats. Women are 700 times more sensitive to the teratogenic effects of thalidomide than are hamsters. You cannot predict in advance whether humans are more or less sensitive to any particular chemical. Thus, there is no option but to test at higher levels than those to which humans are exposed if you are seriously interested in trying to decide whether food additives or drugs, particularly those used for relatively trivial and non-life-threatening causes, are likely to produce cancer, birth defects, or adverse genetic effects.

The idea that any chemical can be made to exhibit carcinogenic properties by testing it at high dosages just is not true. Reports from the International Union Against Cancer, the National Cancer Institute, and the Surgeon General's Ad Hoc Committee on Low Levels of Environmental Carcinogens have never suggested that testing of noncarcinogenic chemicals at high dosages will nonspecifically induce cancer. In the bionetics study sponsored by the National Cancer Institute, approximately 150 industrial chemicals and pesticides, selected on grounds of possible carcinogenicity or other deleterious effects, were tested for carcinogenicity, with commencing exposure in infancy and using maximally tolerated doses. Less than 10 percent of these chemicals proved to be carcinogenic!

It is clear that industry is entitled to know exactly what tests are expected of them. In this respect, the situation would probably be greatly facilitated if protocols were promulgated in the Federal Register together with guidelines for evaluation of resulting data.

As far as epidemiology is concerned, the argument that chemical agents have been used for a long time and that they appear to be safe on the basis of apparent human experience is not reasonable. In between the time of human exposure to chemicals and the resulting cancer, there may be a latent period of ten to thirty years; in addition, it is difficult to isolate the effects of any one chemical in the environment from the masses of other chemicals to which human beings are concurrently exposed, and for which there are no sharp differentials in human exposure.

Even with cigarettes, for example, in studies on humans who previously smoked five packs, four packs, three packs, two packs, or no packs per day and with control groups (e.g., using populations in which there were sharp differentials in exposure) it took several decades to establish a direct causal relationship between cigarette smoking and lung cancer. In the case of chemical products that are widely used or disseminated in the environment, there are no simple ways of demonstrating epidemiological relationships. Hence, the idea that the human experience is a guide to safety is not acceptable.

QUALITY OF THE DATA BASE

Let me return now to the quality of the data base, on which all judgments of safety and benefit must ultimately rest. At the present moment, data are generated by industry, under conditions of obvious direct client constraints, either by industrial scientists or by commercial testing houses. These data are submitted in secrecy to the regulatory agencies and subsequent decisions are made behind closed doors. No mechanisms have been developed, as yet, for involvement of the citizen or consumer or of his scientific and legal representatives in the regulatory decision making process. There is ample evidence of close and intimate associations between regulatory agencies and industry. The top management of the Food and Drug Administration largely has been recruited from industry or from industrial consulting organizations. At retirement senior FDA officials often enter those industries they previously have regulated. Restrictive employment mobility clauses are commonplace in certain industries, and these may prevent any employee leaving a certain industry to take a related job in a competitive industry for some period of time afterwards. We do not have such restricted mobility clauses for senior officials in the FDA, or other regulatory agencies, who came from industry or who may subsequently go to industry.

Closely allied interests have developed between industry and commercial testing houses. Examination of the cyclamate literature indicates that studies sponsored by its manufacturer generally showed that cyclamates are acceptable from a safety viewpoint. Contrastingly, studies sponsored by the Sugar Research Foundation tended to show that cyclamates are harmful.

As far as questions of manipulation of data or the poor quality of the data base are concerned, a few illustrative examples indicate the extent and scope of this problem, as well as how counterproductive poor or questionable data are to long-term industrial interests. In 1967, 50 percent of all petitions submitted to the FDA in support of food additives were rejected by Commissioner Ley because of incomplete, inadequate, and nonspecific data; such decisions are, of course, costly to industry. Fraudulent manipulation of data has been clearly and legally established with drugs such as MER-29, for which officials of Richardson-Merrell Company were criminally convicted; Dornwall, for which Wallace and Tiernan Company were found guilty of submitting false data; Flexin, for which McNeil Laboratories pleaded nolo contendere to charges of willfully concealing information; and Pan-alba, which was withdrawn from the market following discovery by an FDA inspector in March 1969 of secret laboratory files indicating its nonefficacy.

Let us proceed to the Food Protection Committee of the National Academy of Sciences. This is a group to which the FDA in the past twelve years has consistently turned for advice. Let us examine the nature of this committee, its objectivity, social responsibility, and composition. The Food Protection Committee has been strongly supported by grants from the food, chemical, and packaging industries. In April 1969, a nine-man task force of this committee released a report entitled "Guidelines for Estimating Toxicologically Insignificant Levels of Chemicals in Food." Five members of this committee were industrial employees, one was a commercial testing house director, and three were academic scientists with long and intimate relationships with industrial interests. The point about this is that nearly all of these committee members had certain economic commitments to the food industry. It also is important to state that none of the authors of this report are recognized as authorities, let alone as even experienced, in the field of chemical carcinogenesis. This lack of familiarity with the fundamental problems of carcinogenesis, coupled with inherent economic constraints, expressed themselves in views such as, "if a chemical has been used in commerce for five years or more without evidence of overt toxicity, ... it is consistent with sound toxicological judgment to conclude that small amounts in the human diet are toxicologically insignificant." Such viewpoints have been overwhelmingly rejected by the informed scientific community and have been unequivocally condemned in a recent report by the Surgeon General's Ad Hoc Committee on Low Levels of Environmental Carcinogens.

The NAS, I hasten to add, is not unaware of these problems and is apparently developing internal reforms to minimize or obviate such flagrant conflicts of interest. Illustrative of such awareness is the explicit statement of Dean Harvey Brooks, past chairman of the NAS Committee on Science and Public Policy, who stated in 1971: "It is true that some of our bodies -- the Highway Research Board, the Food and Nutrition Board, the Building Research Advisory Board, and the Space Science Board, for instance -- may be constituted too completely with those who have an economic or institutional interest in the outcome of their work." Nevertheless, there has been no apparent recognition by the NAS of the need to elect and involve scientific representatives of public interest and consumer groups in committees concerned with problems of safety and related critical societal issues. Such action would be likely to enhance public confidence in reports by NAS-NRC committees.

The significant influence of economic and related constraints in expert advisory committees, both federal and nonfederal, thus now has become increasingly appreciated. In addition to constraints on the generation of objective data, constraints on the evaluation and interpretation of these data by regulatory agencies may also influence the implications of the data base.

There is a growing consensus of the need for legislation to ensure impartial and competent testing of all products for which human exposure is anticipated. The present system of direct, closed-contract negotiations between manufacturing industries and commercial and other testing laboratories is open to abuse and creates obvious mutual constraints.

One possible remedy would be the introduction of a disinterested advisory group or agency as an intermediary between manufacturers and commercial and other testing laboratories. Proper legal and other safeguards would have to be developed to minimize potential abuses and conflicts of interest. Manufacturers would notify the intermediary group when safety evaluation was required for a particular product. The advisory group would then solicit contract bids on the open market. Bids would be awarded on the basis of economics, quality of protocols, and technical competence. The progress of testing would be monitored by periodic project site visits, as is routine with federal contracts. At the conclusion of the studies, the advisory group would comment on the quality of the data, make appropriate recommendations, and forward these to the concerned regulatory agency for routine action.

This approach appears more consistent with general industrial practice than is the secret award of unbidded contracts. Additionally, quality checks during testing would ensure the high quality and reliability of data, and minimize the need to repeat studies, thus reducing pressure on involved federal agencies to accept unsatisfactory data on a post hoc basis. This approach would not only minimize constraints due to special interests, but would also serve to upgrade the quality of testing in commercial and other testing laboratories.

Additionally, the development of independent nonprofit research centers concerned with problems of consumer, occupational, and environmental safety should be encouraged in an effort to develop constraint-free research. Universities represent such a potential resource, but the requisit concept of interdisciplinary research is relatively novel to most universities, which are still structured on classical department lines. The national laboratories also represent a source of research potential but, under existing charter, they cannot be directly responsive to industrial needs.

PUBLIC ACCESS TO DATA

Further legislation concerning public access to data is critically needed. All formal discussions between agencies, industry, and expert federal and nonfederal committees on all issues relating to human safety and environmental quality, as well as data relevant to such discussions, properly belong in the public domain. Indeed, under the 1967 Freedom of Information Act, all federal records are intended to be open to the public with the exception of specific exemptions such as trade secrets.

In a major policy shift announced May 4, 1972, by Assistant General Counsel Peter Hutt, the FDA proposed making available for public inspection "most of its files and correspondence." Prior FDA policy gave most of the agency's documents confidential status. Under the new policy, it is claimed that all but about 10 percent would be open for inspection. Specifically excluded would be trade secrets, investigations in progress, and internal correspondence.

The FDA proposals are generally regarded as cosmetic by consumer advocates, because "trade secrets" and the other exemptions are defined so broadly that much vital information remains secret. For example, the FDA continues to keep secret the scientific data upon which safety and efficacy of new drugs are decided. It will only release manufacturers' summaries of these data. Anita Johnson of the Health Research Group, Washington, has stated: "The summaries will be perfectly useless. No competent scientist trying to assess the safety or efficacy of a drug would rely on summarized data." Another consumer advocate, James S. Turner, appeared equally unimpressed with Mr. Hutt's new regulations: "All he has done is eliminate some of the FDA's more outrageous restrictions."

Demands for access to data are now being properly extended to internal memoranda and documents which the FDA considers to be exempt from the requirements of the Freedom of Information Act. Recent impetus to these demands has been additionally provided by "leakage" of an internal FDA memorandum, dated September 27, 1972, by Dr. Johnson, Director of Veterinary Medical Review of the Bureau of Veterinary Medicine, which made it clear that the FDA is in serious violation of the law, in that they have allowed and are still allowing use of a wide range of carcinogenic feed additives for cattle, poultry, swine, and sheep in the absence of practicable analytic methods which should be used to detect or exclude any residues in animal foods. The memorandum also emphasized major deficiencies in FDA screening programs for other feed additives, such as antibiotics and pesticides. The author of the memorandum unambiguously stated: "Unless the FDA resolves this drug residue problem, we will soon be in direct confrontation with Congress and the consumers defending an untenable position. For the FDA to ignore this problem would be disastrous." The public health implications of this alarming information were the subject of hearings before the Senate Committee on Commerce on March 21, 1973.

Incidents of this kind have resulted not only in a greater militancy of demands by consumer and public interest groups for unrestricted access to data, on the basis of which decisions may be made that critically affect public health and welfare, but also for demands for public interest involvement in decision making processes to ensure that the rights and welfare of consumers are adequately perceived and appropriately balanced against industrial interests in a societally acceptable manner.

THE PUBLIC INTEREST

In addition to open access of data on all issues of product safety, public health and welfare, and environmental safety, it is important that the consumer and public interest be adequately represented at the earliest stages of the decision making process and agency-industry discussions. Decisions by agencies on technological innovations or on new products after closed discussions on data which have been treated confidentally are unacceptable; similar considerations obtain for products already established in commerce with relation to data on safety and efficacy. The consumer and public interest apart, such decisions are contrary to the long-term goals of industry, which should be protected from perforce belated objections. While there is a growing, if not belated, acceptance of the legitimacy of demands for representation by public interest groups, formal mechanisms for this purpose have not yet been developed in the FDA. However, in January of 1972, senior agency officials began informal informational monthly meetings with leading consumer advocates and representatives.

Reflecting these concerns for representation of the public interest in the regulatory process, two major bills to establish a Consumer Protection Agency (CPA) have been developed. CPA bills S. 707 and H.R. 21 were introduced by Senator Abraham Ribicoff (D-Conn.) on February 1, 1973, and by Representative Chet Holifield (D-Calif.) on January 3, 1973. The Ribicoff Bill is the stronger.

The Holifield Bill has been criticized by consumer advocates, as it limits the proposed CPA to a reactive role with insufficient power to effectively represent the consumer.

While such concerns for consumer safety have been instrumental in developing congressional initiatives for the Consumer Product Safety Commission, established on October 20, 1972, there is no provision for direct consumer and public interest representation in the decision making process of the Commission. Additionally, the rights for individual initiative in asking the Commission to issue, change, or revoke a product-safety rule do not become effective until December 1975. While the Commission may well exert a powerful impact on consumer product safety, it is likely that the public and consumer interest lobby will stimulate additional congressional initiatives to complement and supplement the activities of this new agency.

A new era is dawning in the relationships between the public, as well as its congressional representatives, and industry, regulatory agencies, the scientific community, and expert advisory committees and groups. Decision making processes must be made less autocratic and must be opened to formal public interest representation if we wish to avoid a continuing series of polarizing confrontations between public interest and consumer groups on the one hand, and industry and regulatory agencies on the other hand. The scientific community still has opportunities to develop initiatives in these areas. But as yet there seems to be little appreciation of such pressing needs and, perhaps even more importantly, little appreciation of the need for the scientific community to address higher priorities to the broad concept of the public interest.

* * *

From: Peter Barton Hutt
      Assistant General Counsel
      Food and Drug Division
      Department of Health, Education, and Welfare

The Food and Drug Administration strongly disagrees with the contentions advanced by Dr. Epstein on the safety of food and drugs and the efforts and effectiveness of the governmental regulatory system. Dr. Epstein's statements concerning the federal regulatory process and the statutes administered by the Food and Drug Administration are largely incomplete or inaccurate. His views on the safety of food and drugs represent an extreme position not shared by the consensus of the scientific community or the public.

Dr. Epstein argues that all chemicals should first be proved to be effective. He fails to state that, under present law, food additives are required to be proved to achieve their intended functional purpose, and drugs must be shown to be effective through adequate and well-controlled clinical studies. His statement also thoroughly confuses these two concepts and the way that they are presently enforced.

The National Academy of Sciences' task force report to which he refers was concerned only with new drugs marketed between 1938 and 1962, when the Food and Drug Administration had statutory authority to disapprove marketing solely on the ground of a lack of safety. When Congress provided the Food and Drug Administration with authority to review new drugs for effectiveness, under the Drug Amendments of 1962, a massive reevaluation of those products was undertaken. The NAS found 7 percent of the drugs -- not 60 percent, as Dr. Epstein contends -- and about 19 percent of the claims ineffective. The 60 percent figure used by Dr. Epstein includes drugs found probably effective or possibly effective, and on many of which further testing has been undertaken to make a final determination of effectiveness.

The Food and Drug Administration is now engaged in implementing the results of this review, pursuant to the statutory procedures established by Congress. Our legal authority to conduct this implementation efficiently and effectively has been strengthened recently by four hard-fought Supreme Court decisions.

The Food and Drug Administration has opposed proposed legislation to require that food ingredients (which include all raw agricultural commodities) be shown, in Dr. Epstein's words, to provide "societal benefits." The Food and Drug Administration believes that the government should not dictate the eating habits of its citizens. The law does not, and should not, prohibit snacks and delicacies, much less alcoholic beverages, because they exhibit no essential "benefit" to society. We know of no objective test to determine whether an emulsifier or a stabilizer used to enhance the taste, appearance, or shelf life of a food would pass any such standard.

With respect to safety, the Food and Drug Administration undertook in 1969 a systematic review of the safety of the compounds in the list of generally recognized as safe (GRAS) food ingredients. A package of eleven regulations and notices published in the Federal Register of July 26, 1973 (38 F.R. 20036) outlines the procedures to be followed in this review and solicits the active and full participation of consumers and independent professionals as well as the regulated industry. A new regulation was also proposed in the Federal Register of July 19, 1973 (38 F.R. 19226) attempting to establish, for the first time, a rational scientific basis for determining the acceptability of assay methods used for assuring the absence of drug residues in edible products of food-producing animals.

The internal Food and Drug Administration memorandum on animal drugs to which Dr. Epstein refers was intended to ascertain problems with these products

so that they could be corrected. We are thus criticized for an internal review
designed to put into motion steps that will more adequately protect the public.
As Dr. Epstein knows, but failed to state, implementation of the recommendations
contained in that memorandum was begun before its existence was made known, and
has continued to date.

Dr. Epstein criticized the composition of the Ad Hoc Committee convened by
the Food and Drug Administration to review the safety of FD&C Red No. 2. He contended that two of the individuals selected for the Committee had preconceived
ideas with which he did not agree. In fact, the Committee was selected to provide
a balance of different viewpoints. Presentations to the Committee were made in
open forum, and consumer representatives made a presentation to the Committee.
The full minutes of both the open session and the deliberations of the Committee
were made public. The Committee unanimously concluded -- contrary to Dr. Epstein's
preconceived conclusions -- that gavage was indeed relevant to human consumption
of beverages, but that the animal studies that had been conducted contained serious
flaws. The Committee has now put together new protocols which are about to be
used in additional testing to determine the issue. In short, the scientific discourse permitted by this review process has worked exactly in the way that one
would ideally hope that it should.

The Food and Drug Administration's proposed new Freedom of Information regulations, published in the Federal Register of May 5, 1972 (37 F.R. 9128) and implemented ever since then, represent a massive change in policy. The Food and
Drug Administration now has gone further than any other public agency in releasing
data and information from its files. Dr. Epstein criticizes us for failing to
release trade secret information. He fails to state that, under two separate
statutes enacted by Congress, it is a criminal offense for any Food and Drug

Administration employee to release trade secret information. Since we are prohibited by law from releasing the actual information, we have proposed to release the next best alternative -- accurate summaries.

Dr. Epstein contended that, in fact, we have not changed our policy, and referred to a letter stating that we would release no information on food additives. Upon checking, I learned that the letter to which he referred was dated July 13, 1971 -- fully a year before the proposed regulations were published. His information is therefore out of date. Since May 1972 we have routinely released all safety data on food additives upon request.

Dr. Epstein charges that there are "intimate associations" between regulatory officials and the regulated industry and that consumers are excluded from the decision making process, and thus implies that the regulatory mechanism is suspect or even crooked. He offers nothing but innuendo to support his contentions, and can show no situation in which there have been improper dealing or influence, or indeed in which industry representatives were afforded greater access or consideration than any other interests. This "McCarthyism" tactic must be rejected out of hand.

There is no absence of opportunity for consumer interests to be represented in the Food and Drug Administration's deliberations. If they are unrepresented, it is because of an unwillingness or inability or lack of resources. The Food and Drug Administration has supported Consumer Protection Agency legislation designed to make certain that consumer interests receive as adequate representation on all public issues as any other interests.

Thus, one must be cautious in accepting the extreme views of those who, like Dr. Epstein, contend that the regulatory process is a hopeless failure, accuse government and industry of dishonesty and venality, attack all attempts to improve the system as simplistic and cosmetic in nature, and attempt to panic the public by scare stories that we are all in imminent danger of being poisoned by deadly foods and drugs, without offering assistance or even a constructive suggestion for improving the current system. The Food and Drug Administration welcomes constructive criticism and the participation of anyone who wishes to help improve the system. But we see little point in muckraking purely for the sake of muckraking. Theodore Roosevelt said, on the occasion of laying the corner-stone of the House of Representatives building:

> There is filth on the floor, and it must be scraped up with the muckrake; and there are times and places where this service is the most needed of all the services that can be performed. But the man who never does anything else, who never speaks or writes save of his feats with the muck-rake, speedily becomes, not a help to society, not an incitement to good, but one of the most potent forces of evil.

* * *

From: Samuel S. Epstein, M.D.
        Swetland Professor of Environmental Health
          and Human Ecology
        Case Western Reserve University Medical School
        Cleveland, Ohio

    I regret that Mr. Hutt's emotional and ad hominem

response has failed to deal substantively with any of the

issues raised in my statement.

                        * * *

234

From: Peter Barton Hutt
        Assistant General Counsel
        Food and Drug Division
        Department of Health, Education, and Welfare

Dr. Epstein regrettably started, and chose the tone and level for, this debate. He has repeatedly attacked me and the Food and Drug Administration, charging that we are violating the law, engaging only in "cosmetic" activities, and generally acting in bad faith. He has been informed that many of his specific comments are unsupportable (e.g., we have already removed some new animal drugs from the market that he contends are still on the market) but he continues to make the same charges over and over again. To expect that I would allow this kind of unprincipled nonsense to go unrebutted seems naïve at best.

I would again urge Dr. Epstein, as I have done in the past, to stop using innuendos and conjecture and to stick to facts. We could then work together in the future in assuring effective administration of the law and protection of the public.

* * *

THE PARTICIPANTS

CHAIRMEN

JOHN R. HOGNESS, M.D., is President of the Institute of Medicine, National Academy of Sciences. Former Executive Vice President and later Director of the Health Sciences at the University of Washington, Dr. Hogness is a California native who received his medical training at the University of Chicago and Columbia-Presbyterian Medical Center in New York. He has held numerous academic and administrative posts at the University of Washington, including Medical Director and Dean of the School of Medicine. As an officer and member of numerous governmental advisory boards, Dr. Hogness currently is a member of the President's National Cancer Advisory Board.

DANIEL E. KOSHLAND, JR., is Professor of Biochemistry, University of California, Berkeley. His area of expertise is enzymology and the understanding of regulatory processes in biological systems on which he has published over two hundred scientific papers. He serves on the editorial boards of Science, Journal of Molecular Biology, Journal of Molecular Pharmacology, and Biochemistry. He recently has served as chairman of the Public Policy Committee of the American Society of Biological Chemists and is now the President of that society.

Dr. Koshland has been a Guggenheim Fellow, a delegate to the International Conference on Peaceful Uses of Atomic Energy and a Visiting Fellow of All Souls College of Oxford University. He recently delivered the following honorary lectures: Leo Marion Lecture of the National Research Council of Canada, the Carter Wallace Lectures of Princeton University, Harvey Lecture of the Harvey Society, the Christian Herter Memorial Lecture at New York University, and the Walker Ames Lectures, Washington University. He is a member of the National Academy of Sciences, the American Academy of Arts and Sciences, the American Society of Biological Chemists, and was recently elected an honorary member of the Japanese Biochemical Society.

SPEAKERS

PHILIP HANDLER is President of the National Academy of Sciences. He was elected by the membership of the Academy to be its eighteenth president and the second to serve in a full-time capacity since the founding of the Academy in 1863.

Dr. Handler is a biochemist, most of whose research has been devoted to the study of enzymes. He has been a member of the faculty of the school of Medicine, Duke University since 1939, where he still holds the title of James B. Duke Professor of Biochemistry. Dr. Handler is co-author of Principles of Biochemistry, now in its fifth edition, and editor of Biology and the Future of Man.

236

PETER BARTON HUTT is Assistant General Counsel for the Food and Drug Division of the Department of Health, Education, and Welfare. A graduate of Yale College and Harvard Law School, Mr. Hutt's primary interests during his legal training and since have been the quality of food and drugs available to the consumer and the promotion and enforcement of legislation ensuring the quality of consumer products.

Prior to his present position, which he assumed in 1971, Mr. Hutt was a partner in the Washington law firm of Covington and Burling. In 1965 he was the attorney in the well-known Easter Case, which established the legal basis for treating alcoholism as a disease. Mr. Hutt is a member of the Institute of Medicine.

JOSHUA LEDERBERG is Professor and Chairman, Department of Genetics, Stanford University Medical School, and Director, Kennedy Laboratories for Molecular Medicine. He was educated at Columbia College. He interrupted his medical studies at Columbia in 1946 to collaborate with E. L. Tatum at Yale College on the genetics of bacteria. This work, which underlies much of our present understanding of molecular genetics, was honored with the Nobel Prize in 1958. After completing his Ph.D at Yale, Dr. Lederberg worked at the University of Wisconsin and then joined the Stanford faculty in 1959.

The control of biological weaponry and environmental hygiene in relation to mutation and cancer have been matters of particular concern to Dr. Lederberg and articulated by him in the public media. In 1955 he was among the first to call attention to chemical environmental hazards as being of comparable importance to radioactive contamination. In recent years he has been interested in the interaction of economics and other social sciences with the data of biology and chemistry as applied to rationally optimal policies for technological development and environmental exploitation, especially in the field of human health.

Dr. Lederberg was elected to the National Academy of Sciences at the age of 32. He has received honorary degrees from Yale, Columbia, Yeshiva, the University of Wisconsin, and an honorary M.D. from the University of Turin, Italy. He has served on the National Advisory Mental Health Council, President Kennedy's Panel on Mental Retardation, and as a technical consultant to the World Health Organization and the U.S. Arms Control and Disarmament Administration.

OLIVER H. LOWRY, M.D., is Chairman of the Department of Pharmacology, School of Medicine, Washington University, St. Louis, a position he has held since 1947. Dr. Lowry was Dean of the School of Medicine, Washington University, from 1955-68. He has held positions in the Department of Biological Chemistry at Harvard Medical School and the Division of Physiology and Nutrition of the Public Health Research Institute of New York City. He is co-author of many scientific publications in the fields of electrolyte physiology, quantitative histochemistry, neurochemistry, metabolic control, nutrition and aging.

He is a member of the National Academy of Sciences, the Society for Pharmacology and Experimental Therapeutics, the American Society of Biological Chemists, the American Academy of Arts and Sciences, and the Royal Danish Academy of Science. He received the Midwest Award of the American Chemistry Society, the Merit Award of Northwestern University, the Distinguished Service Award of the Medical Alumni Association of the University of Chicago, the John Scott Award, and the Borden Award of the Association of American Medical Colleges.

JAMES S. TURNER is founder and codirector of Consumer Action for Improved Food and Drugs, an organization which helps to establish consumer groups in each city where the Food and Drug Administration maintains an office. He also is a partner in the law firm of Swankin, Turner and Koch, Washington, D. C.

Mr. Turner has participated in a number of industry and government committees designed to develop better interaction with organized consumers. At present he serves as consumer liaison on the Food and Drug Administration's Bacteriological Vaccine Review Panel. He has served as a consultant to the Heart and Lung Institute of the National Institutes of Health and as a member of the Food Safety Panel of the 1969 White House Conference on Food, Nutrition, and Health.

From 1968-1971, Mr. Turner worked with Ralph Nader in supervising studies of the Food and Drug Administration, the National Institute of Mental Health, and children in relation to the food industry. He is the author of The Chemical Feast: The Nader Report on the Food and Drug Administration.

W. CLARKE WESCOE, M.D., is Vice Chairman of the Board, Sterling Drug, Inc., and President, Winthrop Laboratories Division. He also is active in a wide range of other capacities: as Director of Phillips Petroleum Company and Hallmark Cards; as Chairman of the China Medical Board of New York; and as Trustee of the Samuel H. Kress Foundation, Columbia University, and the Kansas University Endowment Association.

Prior to assuming his present duties with Sterling Drug, Dr. Wescoe was affiliated with the University of Kansas as Dean, School of Medicine, 1952-60; Director, the Medical Center, 1953-60; Chancellor, 1960-69. He is a member of the American Society for Pharmacology and Experimental Therapeutics, the Harvey Society, and the National Cancer Advisory Board.

PANEL FOR INQUIRY

ROBERT McC. ADAMS, Dean, Division of Social Sciences, The University of Chicago, Chairman

IRVING M. LONDON, Director, Harvard-MIT Program in Health Sciences and Technology

FRANKLIN A. LONG, Director, Department of Chemistry and Program on Science, Technology, and Society, Cornell University

MACLYN McCARTY, Vice President and Physician-in-Chief, Rockefeller University

PHILIP MORRISON, Professor, Department of Physics, Massachusetts Institute of Technology

INVITED DISCUSSANTS

H. THOMAS AUSTERN, Senior Partner, Covington & Burling

JOHN J. BURNS, Vice President for Research, Hoffman-La Roche, Inc.

ROBERT B. CHOATE, Chairman, Council on Children, Media and Merchandising

JOSEPH COOPER, Professor of Political Science, Howard University

EMILIO DADDARIO, Director, Office of Technology Assessment

WILLIAM J. DARBY, President, The Nutrition Foundation, Inc.

H. BRUCE DULL, Assistant Director for Programs, Center for Disease Control

SAMUEL S. EPSTEIN, Swetland Professor of Environmental Health and Human Ecology, School of Medicine, Case Western Reserve University

HOWARD H. HIATT, Dean, School of Public Health, Harvard University

RICHARD L. HALL, Vice President, Research and Development, McCormick & Company, Inc.

ANITA JOHNSON, Health Research Group

RUSSELL T. JORDAN, Vice President for Science and Technology, Charles F. Kettering Foundation

ALLEN V. KNEESE, Director, Quality of the Environment Program, Resources for the Future, Inc.

HANS LANDSBERG, Director, Resource Appraisal Program, Resources for the Future, Inc.

HERBERT L. LEY, JR., Medical Consultant

DAVID P. RALL, Director, National Institute of Environmental Health Sciences, National Institutes of Health

LLOYD B. TEPPER, Associate Commissioner for Science, Food and Drug Administration

HARRISON WELLFORD, Consultant, Center for Study of Responsive Law

GENERAL ADVISORY COMMITTEE

ROBERT McC. ADAMS, Dean, Division of the Social Sciences, The University of Chicago, Chairman

ARTHUR M. BUECHE, Vice President, Corporate Research and Development, General Electric Company

ALLAN V. COX, Professor, Department of Geophysics, Stanford University

PETER C. GOLDMARK, President, Goldmark Communications Corporation

JOHN R. HOGNESS, President, Institute of Medicine, National Academy of Sciences

MICHAEL KASHA, Director, Institute of Molecular Biophysics, Florida State University

DANIEL E. KOSHLAND, JR., Professor, Department of Biochemistry, University of California, Berkeley

PHILIP MORRISON, Institute Professor, Department of Physics, Massachusetts Institute of Technology

FRANK PRESS, Chairman, Department of Earth and Planetary Sciences, Massachusetts Institute of Technology

FREDERICK C. ROBBINS, Dean, School of Medicine, Case Western Reserve University

PROGRAM COMMITTEE

DANIEL E. KOSHLAND, JR., Professor of Biochemistry, Department of Biochemistry, University of California, Berkeley, <u>Chairman</u>

IVAN L. BENNETT, JR., Director, New York University Medical Center

JOHN J. BURNS, Vice President for Research, Hoffman-La Roche, Inc.

WILLIAM J. DARBY, President, The Nutrition Foundation, Inc.

CARL DJERASSI, Professor of Chemistry, Department of Chemistry, Stanford University

H. BRUCE DULL, Assistant Director for Programs, Center for Disease Control, Public Health Service

JOHN R. HOGNESS, President, Institute of Medicine, National Academy of Sciences

PETER BARTON HUTT, Assistant General Counsel, Food and Drug Division, Department of Health, Education, and Welfare

C. HENRY KEMPE, Professor and Chairman, Department of Pediatrics, University of Colorado Medical Center

LOUIS C. LASAGNA, Professor of Pharmacology and Toxicology, University of Rochester

JOSHUA LEDERBERG, Professor and Chairman, Department of Genetics, School of Medicine, Stanford University

C. FREDERICK MOSTELLER, Professor of Mathematical Statistics, Department of Statistics, Harvard University

FREDERICK C. ROBBINS, Dean, School of Medicine, Case Western Reserve University

CHAUNCEY STARR, President, Electric Power Research Institute

ACADEMY FORUM STAFF

ROBERT R. WHITE is Director of the Academy Forum. His career has spanned both academe and industry. In 1967, with the merger of Case Institute of Technology and Western Reserve University, Dr. White became the first Dean of the new School of Management at Case Western Reserve University. At the invitation of the President of the National Academy of Sciences, Dr. White took leave from that institution to initiate and develop the Academy Forum.

M. VIRGINIA DAVIS, Administrative Assistant

BETSY S. TURVENE, Editor